We might as well require a man
to wear still the coat which fitted him when a boy,
as to require civilized society to remain
ever under the regimen of their barbarous ancestors.

First Inaugural Address — Thomas Jefferson

The Human Cage:

A Brief History
of Prison
Architecture

Norman Johnston

Published for The American Foundation, Incorporated
Institute of Corrections, Philadelphia, Pennsylvania
by Walker and Company, New York, New York 10019

Contents

The Human Cage:

A Brief History of Prison Architecture

Introduction

In June 1970 the passage of the Part E Amendments to the Safe Streets Act was imminent. These amendments were designed to provide federal monies for the improvement of state and local correctional facilities and programs. The Law Enforcement Assistance Administration of the United States Department of Justice administers the Safe Streets programs. Top officials of that agency, especially its Associate Administrator Richard W. Velde, were determined that these new funds should not be spent to perpetuate antiquated correctional design concepts.

The Law Enforcement Assistance Administration therefore funded three projects on correctional design. Psychologists at the University of California at Davis under Robert Sommer, Ph.D., developed a series of research proposals concerning the effect of various aspects of institutional design upon the confined individual. The Management and Behavioral Science Center at the University of Pennsylvania, directed by Russell Ackoff, Ph.D., prepared a planning instrument to assist in the designing of juvenile detention centers. And thirdly, the Clearinghouse for Criminal Justice Planning and Architecture was established in the Department of Architecture at the University of Illinois. There Fred Moyer, AIA, and Edith E. Flynn, Ph.D., and their associates developed the important document *Guidelines for the Planning and Design of Regional and Community Correctional Centers for Adults.*

At the same time the Law Enforcement Assistance Administration asked the Institute of Corrections of The American Foundation, Incorporated, to undertake two additional projects aimed at widening the knowledge of correctional design. The

first was to prepare a concise history of
the development of prison architecture.
The second was to conduct a "state of
the art" evaluation of contemporary
correctional facilities.

The American Foundation is a privately
endowed nonprofit organization founded
in 1924 by Edward Bok. Since its inception
it has worked at its founder's purpose — to
make representative government more
responsive to the needs of people. During
the last decade corrections — which is a
responsibility of representative government
— has been the major social interest
of the Institute of Corrections, a division
of The Foundation. The Institute and its
staff have devoted considerable attention
over the years to the design of correctional
facilities. The Board of The Foundation
was eager, therefore, to accept the Law
Enforcement Assistance Administration's
invitation and decided to do all the
research and field work at no cost
to the government.

To staff the "state of the art" study, The
Foundation assembled a multidisciplinary
team consisting of architects, psychologists, and persons with considerable
correctional experience. Their primary
research method was direct observation
and on-site evaluations. Scores of field
trips were made by three members of the
research team — a corrections official, an
architect, and a psychologist. A total of
over 100 new correctional institutions
located in 26 states were visited throughout
the country. Usually there was complete
freedom to speak with inmates and staff
individually and in groups. Every possible
attempt was made to observe the
housing, treatment, and work situations
of the inmates, and impressions were
noted and recorded of the overall effect

of the physical structure and its location
on staff, inmates, and program. Architectural plans for the many institutions
were acquired and studied. Thousands of
photographs were taken. Plans of institutions
yet to be built were also examined.
The report describing the findings of that
survey of contemporary correctional
facilities is being published as a
companion volume to this book.

Dr. Norman Johnston, Professor and
Chairman of the Department of Sociology
and Anthropology at Beaver College near
Philadelphia was engaged to do the historical
research on correctional architecture.
Biographical material about Dr. Johnston
is contained in the back of this book. It is
sufficient here to note that he has collected
and studied material on correctional
architecture for nearly a quarter of a
century, and his travels have taken him to
prisons, old and new, all over the world.
He carefully reviewed, for The American
Foundation, the materials in his extensive
collection and prepared this authoritative
history of the development of correctional
architecture. Most of the photographs and
prints used in this book are from Dr.
Johnston's personal collection.

Because any book dealing with architecture
must have visual as well as verbal impact,
The Foundation engaged Sam Maitin,
a graphic artist, to design the book
and provide it with visual clarity.

Wooden Prison Cage in Early French Chateau
from Les Bagnes, *1845*
by Maurice Alhoy

front end papers:
Convicts Exercising at Pentonville Prison
from The Criminal Prisons of London, *1862*
by Henry Mayhew and John Binny

back end papers:
Serving Dinner in a London Boys' Prison
from The Criminal Prisons of London, *1862*
by Henry Mayhew and John Binny

Early Prisons

If we think of a prison as a place where persons are kept involuntarily by some constituted authority, and realize that occasions when this would be temporarily if not routinely expedient must have existed all through history, then it is understandable that we cannot date meaningfully or accurately the earliest use of prisons.[1]

It is sometimes assumed that prisons in early times were exclusively for detention prior to trial rather than for punishment or improvement of the criminal. This seems to be an oversimplification. Apparently imprisonment was usually a prelude to execution, banishment or other various forms of punishment. But it was also used in lieu of these penalties for some political prisoners of high rank, and it was used to coerce payments of debts owed the government or individuals. It seems also to have been used as punishment for some minor offenses as early as the 14th century.[2] There is also considerable evidence that forced labor on public works, which would have required detention of workers, has a long history at least dating back to Roman times.[3]

Early places of confinement were crude structures, seldom built for the use to which they were finally put. They were likely to be strong cages within a fortress or castle enclosure or subterranean portions of public buildings. Although both classical Greece and Rome are reported to have used stone quarries as prisons, and a number of large public prisons existed in Rome for different kinds of offenders,[4] the only place of confinement about which much is known is the Mamertine Prison. Begun about 640 B.C. by Ancus Martius, and later enlarged, it appears to have been a "vast system of dungeons" constructed, for the most part, under the *Cloaca Maxima*, the main sewer of Rome.[5] The construction existing in the late 19th century consisted of two chambers, one below the other. The upper room measured 30 x 22 feet and received light from a hole in the ceiling 16 feet above the floor. The lower chamber, which was reached by means of an aperture in the floor of the room above, was cone shaped with a diameter of 20 feet and was completely dark.

Although there are no reliable descriptions of ancient places of detention, as we approach the late medieval period a clearer picture emerges of the makeshift arrangements for keeping prisoners. The only characteristic which these structures held in common was their substantial, secure nature. Fortresses, castles, the abutments of bridges, town gates, cellars of municipal buildings and even private dwellings had prisoners detained in them. Some fortresses were used primarily for prisoners of state and consequently gained sinister and far-reaching reputations: the Tower of London in England; the Bastille, Vincennes and Bicêtre in France; and Petropavlovsk in Russia, to name but a few. Here prisoners had small apartments and were given some freedom and privileges.

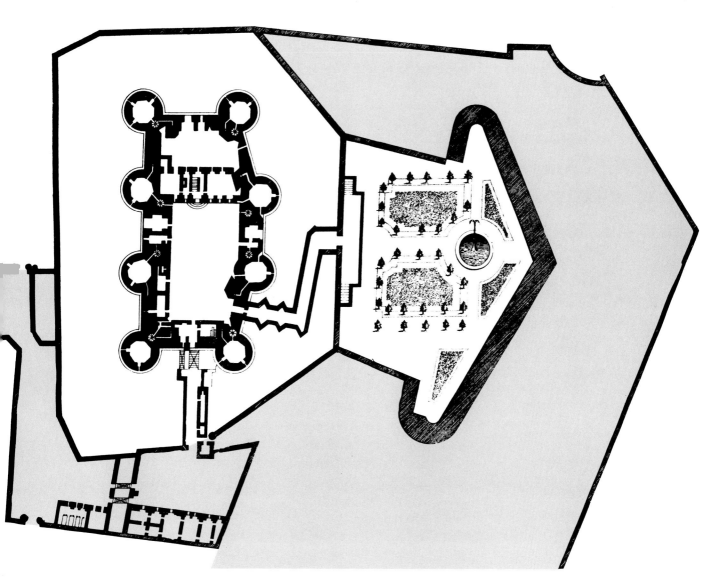

1. The Bastille

Because of the large scale of our contemporary prisons it is difficult for us to conceive of the typical small medieval prison for ordinary criminals awaiting trial or punishment. In spite of the fact that local residents and guides are always ready to point out "dungeons" in castles and fortresses in Europe and the Middle East, these quarters were consigned to nonprison purposes originally. The necessity for storing provisions and siege supplies made space too valuable to be consigned to prisoners. Many medieval prisons were simply ramshackle cages of timber standing in the castle yard or in one of the large halls of the castle keep. Because of their massive nature, lower rooms in castle towers, with but few modifications, were particularly well suited for use as prisons. Specifically constructed prison chambers began to appear more commonly after the 12th century.[6] The massive nature of these tower cells can be seen from the accompanying illustration.

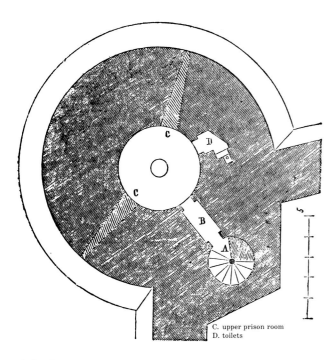

C. upper prison room
D. toilets

2. Castle tower dungeon plan and section

These towers sometimes contained a lighted chamber over an unlighted one, access to which was through a trapdoor in the ceiling. These rooms were usually equipped with a medieval "necessary", a simple toilet cubicle in the thickness of the wall. Dungeons located in the lower stories of castle keeps or in separate underground rooms within the castle enclosure were also relatively common during this period. In many cases the prison was simply a lightless room with very massive walls and perhaps an air shaft and toilet shaft.

With the coming of gunpowder, the military and strategic value of the fortified dwelling began to decline and eventually castles were often used only as dwelling places or as local jails. Such structures with thick, solid walls and partitions, largely windowless for previous defensive purposes and always located in the center of the town, were well suited as stopgap prisons as long as the numbers of inmates continued to be small and their stay relatively brief.

Religious Imprisonment

In searching for the antecedents of both the philosophy of imprisonment as well as the architecture which came to be associated with it, it is necessary to consider briefly the use of imprisonment by the Christian church, especially during the late medieval period. The concept of imprisonment as a substitute for death or mutilation of the body was derived in part from a custom of the early church of granting asylum or sanctuary to fugitives and criminals. Begun largely during the reign of Constantine, this ancient right existed earlier among Assyrians, Hebrews and others. The church at that time had under its aegis a large number of clergy, clerks, functionaries, monks and serfs, and, except the latter, most of these fell under the jurisdiction of the church courts. Traditionally forbidden to shed blood and drawing on the Christian theme of purification through suffering, these canon courts came to subject the wrongdoer to reclusion and even solitary cellular confinement, not as punishment alone, but as a way of providing conditions under which penitence would most likely occur.

Confinement in one's own monastic room, cubicle or little house was mildest of the possible punishments available to the abbot, though little evidence exists as to how extensively it was used. Some of the monastic quarters provided totally separate facilities for each monk[7] so that it was a simple matter to lock up an errant brother for brief periods.

As "mother houses" of monastic orders had satellite houses often located in less desirable places, it was also the practice to transfer monks for varying periods of time to such locations. There is some evidence that some of these satellites came to be regarded as punitive facilities.

For more serious offenses, as early as 500 or 600 A.D., inmates or serfs were placed in prison rooms specifically designated for that purpose. Some orders were more severe than others. Statutes of the order of Cluny specified that the prison must be without door or window, the only entrance being in the middle of the vaulted ceiling, through which a ladder could be lowered. Sometimes prisoners were in irons and seldom was light, heat or wine provided. Although such quarters were on occasion underground, not much is actually known about the appearance of these church prisons. It is not likely that there were ever very many persons confined in them, even in the largest abbeys, and probably only one or two rooms were provided specifically for imprisonment. More than one prisoner must have been confined in some rooms. The 12th century prison in Durham Abbey was a 10 x 20 foot vaulted room with an adjoining chamber containing a latrine and a sort of hatch for passing food to the occupants.[8] In Eastern Europe, especially Austria and Russia, monastic prisons with a larger number of underground cells continued to be used well into the 20th century.

Aside from monastery prisons, every seat of church government, episcopal palace and the like, contained prisons. One of the most famous structures in France is Mont St. Michel, which has served successively as an ecclesiastical, civil and military prison. The citadel was built between the 11th and 14th centuries, and although it was subjected to extensive mutilation and restoration, two small cells known as the "Twins" still exist on the lower level of the Abbey. Directly above them was the ecclesiastical court in the abbot's residence. The jailer's job was made relatively simple as circular trapdoors in the floor gave access to the two cells below. These cells are about 10 x 15 feet and remain nearly dark, light and air coming from a narrow slit piercing the thick exterior walls. Each cell has a small niche in the wall with a hole in the floor as a latrine.

A third type of ecclesiastical prison was exemplified by the prisons built during the Inquisition. Some were newly built, others adapted from already existing structures. Almost no reliable information is available on these structures. Quarters for those imprisoned for life were usually in single rooms underground.[9] Sometimes they were completely dark. The church prison at Goa, Portuguese India, built in the 1600s, consisted of a complex of buildings each two stories high, containing a total of about 200 separate cells. A corridor ran the length of the buildings with seven or eight cells on each side. On one side, cells were about 10 x 10 feet, some with a small barred, unglazed window in the vaulted ceiling. The cells on the other side were dark, somewhat smaller and lower. Walls 5 feet thick separated these rooms, each of which was entered through a set of double doors with space between so that one could be locked before the other was unlocked. The inner door was heavily reinforced with iron latticework and had an opening for food and clothing to be passed into the cell.

The influence of these various types of ecclesiastical prisons upon latter-day penology is difficult to assess. Frequently the philosophy must have been misunderstood or ignored by prison keepers. However, there can be no question as to the Christian religious influence upon the later workhouse movement. All in all, the church dogma of reformation of prisoners left upon later thought and social theory a strong imprint that would be hard to deny.

In contrast, the architecture of the monastic and church prisons was relatively undeveloped, perhaps because the tomblike prison rooms already expressed so well the philosophy of treatment which stressed solitude, suffering, and purification of the soul through mortification of the body. The ascetic Christian dogma, concerned almost exclusively with the well-being of the soul as a preparation for the afterlife, could hardly be expected to bring forth an architecture giving much attention to the physical comforts of the prisoners.

Although church prison architecture seemed to differ little from other prisons of the time, it did undoubtedly inspire the regular use of the cell in civil prisons at a later date when large numbers of criminals, no longer killed or mutilated, first began to be confined as punishment. Thus the system of cellular imprisonment in force for the last 200 years must be regarded as the indirect outgrowth of these uses of imprisonment by the church.

Prisons and the Workhouse Movement Prior to 1780

The breakup of feudalism, coupled with the enclosure movement, resulted in growing social disorder and unrest in Europe during the centuries following the medieval period. This was accompanied by a large increase in the number of vagrants, prostitutes and petty criminals of all sorts. The new humanitarian spirit of the times demanded less sanguinary treatment for these minor offenders than had heretofore been in force. The answer of the 16th century was the workhouse or house of correction, an institution built around the idea of the rehabilitative value of regular work and the formation of "habits of industry". In 1557 the famous London Bridewell was opened, and its motley collection of prisoners was housed in a converted royal palace. Other English towns followed suit and in 1576 Parliament passed an act calling for each county to erect its own "bridewell".

In 1596 a house of correction was set up in Amsterdam for petty offenders. Within a few years other such establishments were opened in other cities in Holland and Germany. The Dutch houses of correction, rather than the earlier English institutions, were to exert a pervasive influence in Belgium and Scandinavia, and possibly also in Spain and Italy.[10]

Through descriptions of the English reformer John Howard, these "bettering houses" of Holland became models for some of the legislation and reform in both Britain and the colony of Pennsylvania.

Although the principles of these houses of correction represented a significant departure from older methods of treatment, the architecture revealed no break from the past. Workhouses were frequently in the form of a hollow square, much as the hospitals and convents of the time. In fact, many were located in buildings once used for such purposes. Prisoners worked and slept in common rooms, although the youthful recalcitrants committed by their well-to-do parents might be lodged in private rooms.

Of the many jails and workhouses built in Europe during the 1600s and 1700s, only a few can be said to have possessed either a distinctive architectural form or a method of treatment which would set them apart from the other institutions of the time. But these few were to have great influence on the reforms of the following 100 years.

3. Juvenile House of Correction of San Michele, Rome, 1704

The use of cellular confinement in the modern sense is usually traced to the famous *casa di correzione* established in the hospice of San Michele in Rome in 1704. Although

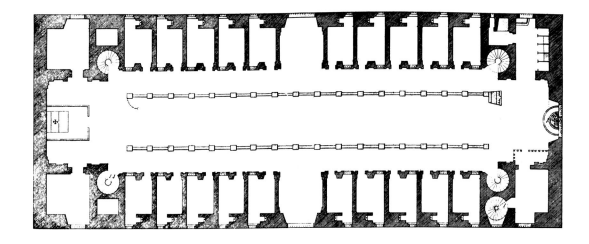

there were earlier examples of cellular confinement,[11] San Michele was probably influenced more by the knowledge papal authorities possessed concerning the Dutch workhouses. The architect, Carlo Fontana, designed a rectangular structure with 30 outside rooms or cells arranged on three tiers with balconies or galleries on each level. Each cell contained a mattress and had a latrine, an outside window, and a solid door with a small aperture opening onto the balconies, which could be closed from without by a small covering. These sleeping rooms faced a large center hall which was used as a workroom, dining room and a chapel.

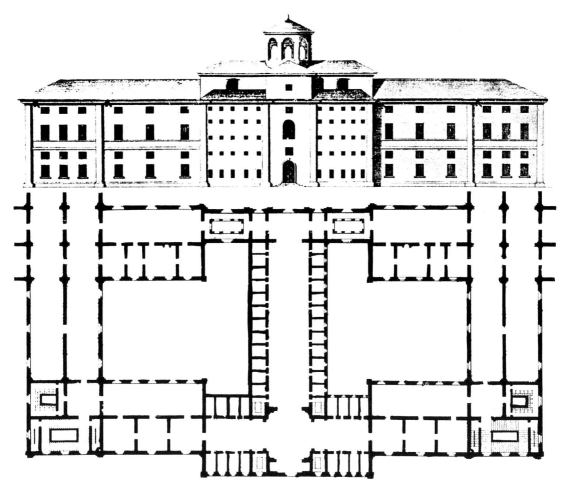

4. Milan House of Correction, c.1756

The boys, with leg chains, worked in silence manufacturing articles for the Vatican state.

Another 18th century Italian institution worthy of note was the Milan House of Correction, built in the late 1750s or early 1760s. The general design combined elements of the San Michele plan with the traditional cross plans found in Italian churches and hospitals of that period. The *T*-shaped main building contained 120 sleeping rooms about 9 x 8 feet arranged along the outer walls on three levels and connected by stone galleries. One wing housed men, one wing boys and one was used as an infirmary and for women prisoners. The prisoners worked in the large corridor between the cells, which measured 124 x 31 feet.

The unsettled economic and social conditions which gave rise to the English and Dutch workhouses continued to plague Austrian Flanders, which found itself burdened with vagabonds, beggars and petty thieves. Consequently, in 1772 the government, under the Empress Maria Theresa, began building a remarkable house of correction in Ghent. The principles applied in its management were certainly not new but probably in combination had never been put into practice: night isolation of prisoners, separation of the sexes and separation of prisoners of the same sex according to categories based on age, degree of criminality, and length of sentence.

Architecturally Ghent can be regarded as the first large-scale penal institution in which a conscious attempt was made to bring architecture to the aid of the treatment philosophy. The sources of inspiration for the truly original design of this prison are not known. The plan was in the form of a giant octagon formed by eight trapezoid-shaped units, each completely self-contained to allow for the separation of various classes of prisoners as well as to facilitate construction of the prison in stages as funds became available. Each unit was to have sleeping cells and workshops back to back with such facilities in adjacent units. Each unit was to be reserved for a specific type of offender. The central octagonal court formed by the inner sides of the various units was to be flanked by service facilities. In spite of its later deterioration, the *maison de force* at Ghent was initially a highly original and advanced institution, both in terms of treatment and architecture. Although its peculiar design had few direct imitators, the spirit of that architecture and of the management of the prison was to have many ramifications in later reforms.

These three institutions just described — Milan, Rome and Ghent — must be regarded as exceptional prisons. They received considerable favorable publicity by being described and pictured in John Howard's influential account of his prison visits, *State of the Prisons,* which went through a number of editions in the late 18th century. However it would be misleading to leave this period without describing the more ordinary prisons being built at the time. It must be remembered that from the 16th century onwards, an increasing number of petty offenders were being placed in prisons in lieu of corporal and capital punishment or forced labor. The older places of temporary confinement proved both too small for the numbers of prisoners and also extremely unhealthy. Prisoners even in jails built for the purpose were placed in large rooms, with little attempt to separate the sexes, adults from children, hardened offenders

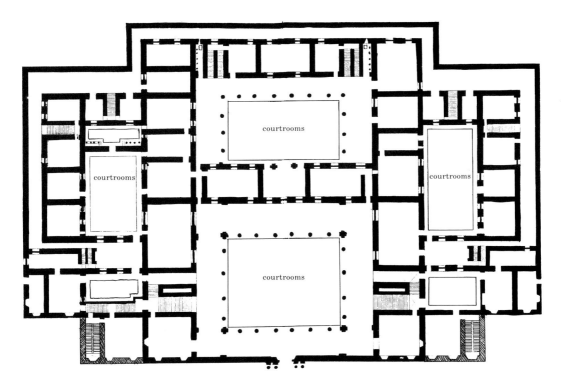

5. New Jail, Milan, 1624. Typical rectangular prison with congregate facilities.

6. Newgate Prison, London

from the more naive, or the sick from the healthy. There was no heat nor glass in the windows, seldom sufficient water and usually little, if any, food for those without money. Some prison rooms had no sewers or water or bedsteads. These conditions as well as terrible overcrowding[12] led to their constant depopulation through "jail fever" or typhus. The use of irons and chains, the system of charging inmates fees for various services and the great amount of exploitation of inmates by fellow inmates still further aggravated the situation.

Architecturally these prisons showed no characteristic form. The larger prisons in London, Paris, Rome and other European cities consisted only of a series of strong rooms and courts for exercise, with little attempt to separate different types of prisoners or to supervise them. The old engraving shown here of a common room at Newgate in London must portray a rather characteristic prison scene during the 17th and 18th centuries.

Smaller prisons consisted of one or several large rooms and occasionally individual cells for troublesome inmates. Sometimes these rooms were underground, as those at the Wood Street Compter in London and the Warwick County Jail.[13]

During the development of penal philosophy up to the end of the 18th century, it seems that no generally accepted principles prevailed. A few outstanding pioneer prisons served as models for later reforms — the architecture being easier to duplicate than the internal regimen — and the early philosophy of work, religious meditation and solitary contemplation, evolved first in the monastic prisons and later in the workhouses, was to have a rebirth during the reforms of the late 18th century. Little more was expected of the master builders of this early period than that they make the prison rooms secure. Early architects like Vitruvius apparently had little interest in prisons. But later, some writers began to make suggestions on the style of prisons. A Spanish writer of the 16th century, for example, suggested: "The jail has to be formed out of rough stones in order to appear fearsome, but in such a manner that the prisoners are not deprived of the light of the sky...."[14] Francesco Milizia, in his *Principj di architettura civile*, published in 1785, sets forth the now familiar principle that the form of a prison must go along with its purpose. Melancholy should be seen in the civil prisons. In the institutions for the more serious offenders, the style should be heavier — "... high and thick walls with savage-like appendages which throw forth the most horrible shadows", "uninviting and cavern-like entrances", and "frightful inscriptions". Everything, in short, must inspire "darkness, threatening, ruins, terror" which, the writer felt, would control crime among the citizens.[15]

Although there was some agreement on the general quality of the prison exterior among the writers, in reality a prison architecture, in the sense of a distinctive external appearance and the interior arrangement different from other types of buildings, had not yet come into being. Following the workhouse movement in the 16th century, it is true that prisons were increasingly built as prisons. But with very few exceptions, their style and arrangement varied little from that of other buildings of the same size. One might say that neither a coherent penal philosophy nor a self-conscious architecture of prisons had yet emerged at the point in the 18th century that John Howard began his great inquiries into prison conditions and prison buildings.

Prison Reform from 1780 to the American Influences

The workhouses, local prisons and houses of correction built in Britain and on the Continent during the 17th and 18th centuries with such sanguine expectations had badly deteriorated by the last half of the 18th century. The public awareness of the shocking conditions in these institutions started a reform movement in England in the 1780s that spread to the Continent and the Americas. To a remarkable extent it was set in motion by the labors of one unassuming man, John Howard. Howard traveled extensively, visiting all the jails and prisons of Britain and the more important ones all over Europe, some as far away as Russia and the south of Italy. His detailed observations appeared in successive editions of his *State of the Prisons*, first published in 1777.

The operation of jails and prisons at that time was often a sinecure, a moneymaking operation for a particular official who had no government funds to run his institution. As a consequence, buildings were in disrepair, living quarters were incredibly crowded and unsanitary, prisoners were rarely provided with food and had little means of keeping clean. Howard was struck by the almost complete lack of supervision and control over prisoners. Shakedowns and assaults were common and the more sophisticated inmates freely corrupted the younger and more naive.

In Britain especially, public attention and debate about prison matters following these disclosures led, if not yet to a coherent penal philosophy, certainly to a more detailed consideration of prison construction than had ever occurred before. As the prisons were beginning to accommodate large numbers of prisoners, while only a decade earlier similar offenders were being sent to the gallows, imprisonment was, of course, expected to punish. But it was abundantly clear from Howard's writings and subsequent parliamentary committee testimony that prisoners influenced one another in ways that made reformation unlikely. As individual celling was seldom tried during this period because of the cost and inconvenience, the alternative was great reliance upon careful and continual surveillance by the guards and governor over the prisoners in their yards, workrooms, and in some cases, living quarters. This was strengthened by an often elaborate system of classification which separated the inmates into various classes within the prison. Constant, unseen inspection became the *sine qua non* of good jail design and administration, the mechanism whereby the prison setting could be freed of its old abuses and the prisoners protected from corruption and disruptive behavior. The other great concern of the reformers was the health of the prisoners. Within the limits of the medical knowledge of the times and the general standards in the civilian population, there was a great concern for proper toilet facilities, baths, a piped supply of clean water, covered sewers and an infirmary. Because epidemics were thought to stem from impure air or "miasmas" rather than contagion, proper ventilation of buildings and their location were given much attention.

Based on these considerations, a number of different arrangements were worked out by architects, court officials, prison directors, as well as by master builders and stone masons who sometimes designed prison structures. Layouts fell into three main groups: the rectangular form based for the most part upon the older 18th century jails and earlier ecclesiastical buildings; the circular forms, including various polygonal arrays; and the radial, by far the most prevalent from 1790 onwards in Britain. Considerable impetus was given to innovation by the technology of the newly-evolving industrial and scientific revolutions. The increasing structural use of cast iron was of particular value to prison designers. The decreasing cost of iron made its extensive use for bars, doors, door jambs, and even floors and walls, feasible for the first time. New developments in the central heating and ventilating of large buildings, and the use of plumbing were to find some of their first applications in the prisons of this period.

One need give little attention to the first type of prison, built in the form of a hollow square, simple rectangles or *H* shapes. Although they were much superior to their predecessors in terms of both security and health, these plans were criticized for two main reasons: they seldom provided for proper separation of prisoners of various classes and their arrangement of cells and workrooms made it impossible to observe properly the prisoners in the continuous fashion expected at that period.

The truly original and characteristic forms that developed in the late 18th and early 19th centuries were the circular, polygonal and radial plans, which might be regarded as whimsical architectural aberrations were it not for the fact that they became so prevalent. Space does not permit a discussion of the classical formalism in architecture which found expression in geometric patterns both in the interior plans of buildings as well as their arrangement in great monumental arrays such as Versailles and Washington,

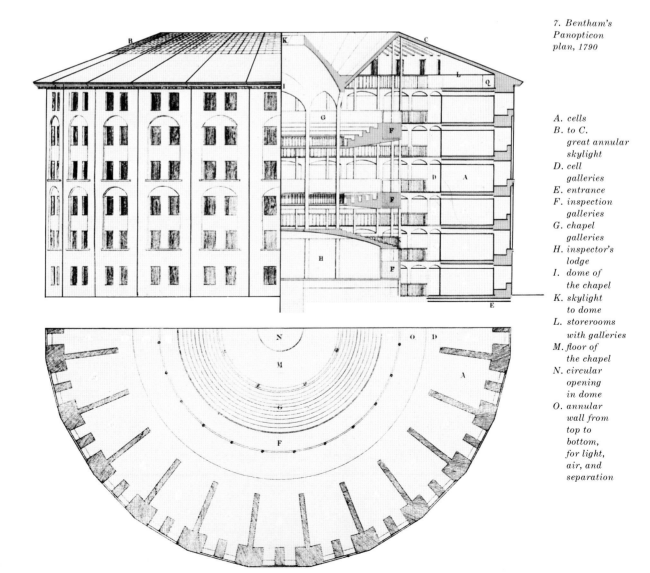

7. Bentham's Panopticon plan, 1790

A. cells
B. to C.
  great annular skylight
D. cell galleries
E. entrance
F. inspection galleries
G. chapel galleries
H. inspector's lodge
I. dome of the chapel
K. skylight to dome
L. storerooms with galleries
M. floor of the chapel
N. circular opening in dome
O. annular wall from top to bottom, for light, air, and separation

D.C., or in the military architecture of the Renaissance. Nevertheless this legacy was very strong in the backgrounds of the architects responsible for these new geometric prison plans.

Although many examples could be cited of early circular buildings, the most forceful exponent of the circular form for prisons was the 18th century criminal law reformer, social philosopher and political economist Jeremy Bentham. At the time he proposed his *Panopticon* prison, Bentham was at the height of his distinguished career. His direct inspiration for a circular prison came out of a trip he made to Russia in 1787 to visit his brother, Samuel, who was an

8. Illinois State Penitentiary, near Joliet, 1916–1924

9. Interior Panopticon cellhouse, Illinois State Penitentiary, Stateville, Near Joliet

engineer in the service of Prince Potemkin, prime minister of Catherine the Great. Samuel was constructing a circular textile mill, so arranged that the workers could be observed by supervisors in the center whom they could not see. For 20 years Jeremy Bentham wrote, talked, and maneuvered to get the British government to allow him to build and manage his proposed circular penitentiary, termed by Aldous Huxley a "totalitarian housing project".[16] George III, whom Bentham thought regarded him as a radical, never permitted the prison to be built. Bentham's scheme, remarkably advanced for the time, consisted of a very large circular building of cast iron and glass containing cells on several tiers around the periphery. The cells were to have barred fronts, and to be heated in winter and artificially cooled in summer by means of air forced over ice and directed through flues into the cells. Speaking tubes would connect each cell with the keeper's tower in the center. By these means the keeper in his louvred tower could carry out continuous, and unseen surveillance both visual and auditory over the inmates.

Although the *Panopticon* penitentiary was never erected in Britain, several circular institutions were later built in Spain (1852) and in the 1880s at three locations in Holland. In the 20th century the cell buildings and dining room at the

10. Horseshoe-shaped Virginia Penitentiary, Richmond, 1797–1800

Illinois Penitentiary near Joliet, and the model prison on the Isle of Pines off Cuba were faithful reproductions of Bentham's plan but on a larger scale. The Cuban institution, opened in 1926, had a capacity of 5,000 and was enclosed only by a wire fence. A circular mess hall is surrounded by cellhouses with five tiers of outside cells which open onto balconies on each level. There are no walls or bars between cell and balcony. The most recent example of the circular plan is the central portion of the Badajoz Provincial Prison in Spain that opened in 1952.

A large number of semicircular prisons were built in Ireland, Scotland and England and several on the Continent in the 30 years following the *Panopticon* proposal, in most cases either directly or indirectly influenced by Bentham's efforts. The *D*-shaped Edinburgh House of Correction contained 129 "sleeping closets" and 52 much larger "working cages". At the center of the half circle was a "dark apartment...from which the governor or his deputy without being themselves visible, can see at a glance what is doing in all parts of the house."[17] Although this institution was roofed over between inspection tower and cells, most jails were not, and in fact the original degree of surveillance intended by Bentham was usually quite impossible.

In the United States two early examples illustrate the difficulties of achieving good visual surveillance once the original *Panopticon* plan is modified significantly. The Virginia Penitentiary in Richmond was planned by Thomas Jefferson and Benjamin Latrobe with some inspiration from French and British sources. Opened in 1800, the prison was horseshoe-shaped, with cells opening onto covered arcades on four levels. Originally the ends were joined by a wall, with a warden's house in the center.

The second institution was William Strickland's Western Penitentiary designed in 1818 and erected outside Pittsburgh. The architect, who was trained by Latrobe, built a ringlike structure with cells back to back opening onto covered arcades. The inner yard of the prison was not roofed over and was cut up by walls into smaller areas in such a way that neither range of cells could be properly observed. In addition the cells were totally inadequate for solitary confinement and work so that the whole structure had to be torn down seven years after its opening.

We have seen how the reformers of the late 18th century demanded more prisons of a different character and how this resulted in not only a continuation of the use of the older rectangular forms, but also innovations taking the form of circles, half-circles or polygons. Although such structures were prevalent in Britain, it was another form, the cross, which predominated there and was eventually to lead to the radial or star-shaped arrangements which would finally prevail in Europe. The antecedents of cross-shaped

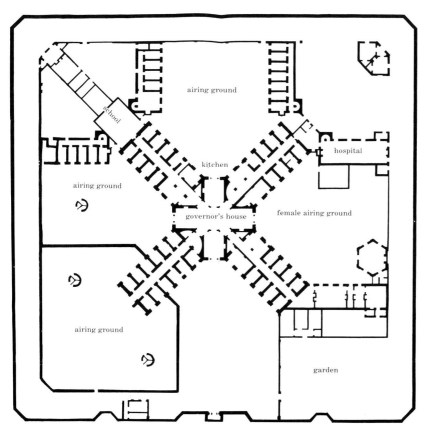

*11. Blackburn's
Suffolk
County Jail,
Ipswich,
England,
1784–1790*

airing ground

school

hospital

kitchen

airing ground

female airing ground

governor's house

airing ground

garden

buildings are not hard to trace. Joseph Furttenbach in
works published in 1628 and 1635 presented plans for hospitals, arsenals, schools and lazarettos in cross forms. Aside
from the Greek cross and *X*-shaped arrays, multiple wings
radiating from a central hub were also seen, especially in
"lunatic asylums".

If any single architect can be said to be the father of the

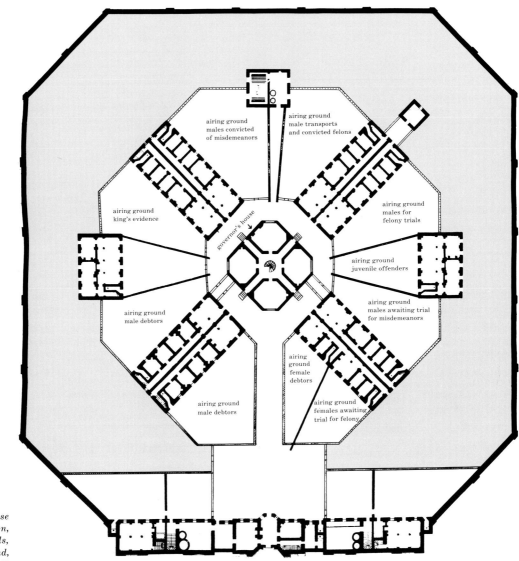

airing ground
males convicted
of misdemeanors

airing ground
male transports
and convicted felons

airing ground
king's evidence

governor's house

airing ground
males for
felony trials

airing ground
juvenile offenders

airing ground
males awaiting trial
for misdemeanors

airing ground
male debtors

airing
ground
female
debtors

airing ground
male debtors

airing ground
females awaiting
trial for felony

*13. Suffolk House
of Correction,
Bury St. Edmunds,
England,
1803–1805*

radial prison plan, this honor must surely go to a now-forgotten London architect, a friend and advisor of John Howard, William Blackburn. Little is known about him but it is clear that during the last five years of his life (d.1790) he was responsible for the construction of 18 jails and prisons in Britain. Blackburn experimented with different arrangements of cell buildings around a centrally-placed governor's house: fan-shaped arrays, Greek crosses, a central hall flanked by two wings, a multiangled building in a half-circle around the governor's house, etc.

The first cruciform jail to appear in Britain was probably his Suffolk County Jail at Ipswich (1784–1790), which was also the first such type whose plan permitted visual inspection of corridors from a central vantage point. An idea of the scale of these little radial jails can be had from the photograph of the house of correction at Abingdon (1804–1812). Although three-story wings were not common at the time, the length of the wings was quite typical.

Most of Blackburn's prisons and in fact those designed by other architects differed from the Ipswich plan in that the center structure was detached from the radiating wings, which were 10 to 30 feet away. Often the wings were joined to the center on the upper floors by means of cast iron bridges. The Suffolk house of correction at Bury St. Edmunds (1803–1805) was typical of such plans. The keeper's house was in the center for surveillance, but the interior of the wings could only be seen by looking in the peepholes at the near ends of the cellblocks. Generally different classes of prisoners were kept in different blocks. As the cell wings were characteristically divided by a wall down the middle, quite elaborate systems of classification and separation of prisoners were possible. Some of these early radial prisons were laid out in complicated fashion, largely to accommodate larger numbers of prisoners. The county jail and penitentiary for Kent at Maidstone (1816–1818) consisted of four clusters with either three or four wings radiating

14. Petite Roquette
Prison, Paris,
1826–1836

from a hub, with a total of 15 wings. Each wing had a dividing wall down the middle, making 30 divisions to hold various types of prisoners.

During the period under consideration, 1780 to 1840, many books and pamphlets continued to be published by the London Society for the Improvement of Prison Discipline, the chief lobbying group for the prison reformers. These printed materials, along with similar publications from other countries, contained careful descriptions and detailed plans of existing institutions but more especially model plans. The best architects of the period devoted themselves to designing prisons, and public competitions were common. By 1826 a government publication could state:

> ...we consider the advantages of the radiating plan to be now so completely established in preference to those of any other, that we should not feel ourselves justified in reporting favorably on a proposed plan of a new county gaol founded on any other principle.[18]

Although these radial prisons were most numerous in Britain, they can occasionally be found on the Continent during this period. The Moscow District Prison, in a Greek cross plan, dates from the first years of the 19th century. The Geneva Penitentiary (1822) consisted of two wings attached to a hub building. In the Kingdom of the Two Sicilies, at Palermo a prison was built between 1834 and 1840. One group of cell buildings consists of three detached wings radiating from a ringlike center building; the other has five wings in a fan shape but with no center building. The prison is still in use. The famous Petite Roquette Prison in Paris (1826–1836), still in operation, has a layout consisting of a complicated combination of six radial wings within a hexagon, forming thereby six pentagonal courts. The prison at Rio de Janeiro (1831–1833) also was influenced by the English radials and consisted of four cellblocks detached from a center building, each divided by a wall down the center.

Reading between the lines of published descriptions and official reports, one suspects that the opportunities for observation of the prisoners were not all that the architect must have envisioned or the magistrates assumed, and that in many cases as little supervision of prisoners took place in 1820 as Howard had found in 1780. Commenting on these earlier plans after Britain had embarked on its ambitious program of building large-scale radial prisons after 1840, Sir Joshua Jebb, the Surveyor-General of Prisons, had this to say:

There is a great apparent facility for inspection; but when its extent is ascertained, it is found to be confined to the exercising yards lying between the buildings. The greatest possible neglect, disorder, and irregularity either on the part of the Officers, or Prisoners, may be going on within the narrow passages, dayrooms, and cells, without anyone being cognizant of it, unless additional superintendence were maintained in each distinct portion of the prison.[19]

We have been considering almost exclusively the *layouts* of jails and prisons, to the exclusion of most of the other things which make up "architecture" as it is ordinarily considered. Concerning the kinds of facilities included in these early jails, it should be noted that cells were generally small, lighted and ventilated only by a small window with thick iron bars. There were no toilets or water taps in the cells. Doors were traditionally wooden with small apertures for viewing the interior of each cell. All walls were of stone with cells usually barrel vaulted. Occasionally hot air furnaces were located in the lower stories or stoves in the corridors on each level. Each prison had by this time an infirmary and workshops. The center building usually contained the governor's quarters below and a chapel above, access to which would be by means of iron bridges to the cell buildings.

Most of the writers on prisons have from the very earliest had definite ideas concerning what should be the general appearance and appropriate style for jails and prisons. It was generally agreed that the style should not be ornate, and there has been continual criticism down to the present time of the elaborateness and pretentiousness of some prison exteriors. But appearance was thought to be much more than just a matter of economy and security. It was expected to be appropriate to the purposes of a prison, and further, to play an active part in carrying out the functions of imprisonment itself, namely, that of deterrence of the inmates and the general public. An encyclopedia article of 1826 expresses such a philosophy of design in highly enthusiastic terms:

The style of architecture of a prison is a matter of no slight importance. It offers an effectual method of exciting the imagination to a most desirable point of abhorrence. Persons, in general, refer their horror of a prison to an instinctive feeling rather than to any accurate knowledge of the privations or inflictions therein endured. And whoever remarks the forcible operation of such antipathies in the vulgar, will not neglect any means however minute, of directing them to a good purpose. The exterior of a prison

*15. Gothic prison
facade in
Leicester,
England, 1825*

*should, therefore, be formed in the heavy and sombre style,
which most forcibly impresses the spectator with gloom
and terror. Massive cornices, the absence of windows or
other ornaments, small low doors and the whole structure
comparatively low, seem to include nearly all the points
necessary to produce the desired effect. Our own Newgate
perhaps embodies these as perfectly as can be desired.*[20]

Architects experimented with different motifs as well
as styles: the Kilmainham Prison in Dublin, opened in 1796,
had a pair of coiled serpents above the doorway. George
Dance's Newgate in London, erected in 1770 and rebuilt in
1784, had festooned chains above the main gate.

The revolt against reason and formalism which characterized the Romantic Movement in literature as well as
architecture found expression in the revival of various
period styles in the 19th century—Gothic, classical Greek
and Roman, Italianate, Tudor, etc.—in what Nikolaus
Pevsner has called the "fancy-dress ball of architecture".
Before 1790 it was unusual to find a prison erected *as a
prison,* and when it was, there was little inside or out to
distinguish it from any other large building. But in the early
19th century architects were reaching into the ready grab-
bag of period styles for one appropriate to a prison. But

which? The Greek Revival, usually Doric, or a castellated style involving Gothic details were the most common choices, although more straightforward styles have sometimes been employed.

The Gothic, because of its obvious ornateness, received some criticism. Although its appearance was simple compared with later prisons and the size of the structure relatively modest, even the Liverpool Borough Jail was criticized on both these counts when it was completed. A descriptive work on the city published in 1793 had this to say about Blackburn's prison:

> This temple of the goddess Laverna is situated at the northern extremity of the town, where it rises in all the glare of ostentatious majesty. A stranger, on being informed it is the common jail, must be immediately prejudiced by a very indifferent opinion of the honesty or reputed wealth of a place which required a building for the reception of villany and insolvency that covers more than twice the ground occupied by the prison of Newgate and on fair calculation will hold half the inhabitants of Liverpool.... a distant view indicates a magnificent castle. The pile is enormous; the materials of which it is composed would build a village.[21]

And even as early as 1789 John Howard had written:

> The new gaols, having pompous fronts, appear like palaces to the lower class of people in Ireland; and the same persons object to them in this account, especially those who are obliged to contribute towards their expence, and think it would be better if they were less commodious.[22]

Systems Develop and Compete in the 19th Century

In tracing innovations in prison architecture thus far, attention has been focused exclusively on Europe, and, in the decades between 1780 and 1820, particularly on Great Britain. But at this juncture the development both of coherent philosophies of imprisonment and characteristic related architecture was taking place in North America, especially in Pennsylvania. It was no accident that prison reforms blossomed so soon and so well in this colony. Beginning with William Penn's revolutionary penal code of 1682, Pennsylvania Quakers continuously pressed for penal reform. The first prison of any consequence to come from their efforts was the Walnut Street Jail, opened the year the Rev-

16. Haviland's
Eastern
Penitentiary,
Philadelphia,
1821–1836

olution broke out. Although a model in its early days, its architecture was quite ordinary. While a small "penitentiary house" was built in the yard of the prison for solitary confinement as regular treatment, it was apparently used mostly for disciplinary purposes. The remainder of the prisoners lived in congregate cells, which very soon became greatly overcrowded.

Wrestling with the same obvious flaws in their prisons which Howard and other reformers had identified in Britain, the Pennsylvania Quakers gradually forged their philosophy of total isolation of each prisoner night and day. Solitude would serve several purposes: it would be punishment *par excellence,* but more importantly, it would give a man time for reflection and contrition and protect the naive from contamination by the more sophisticated, preventing also plots, escapes and attacks on keepers, which were at the time most prevalent. Religious instruction, work in the cell and visits by philanthropically inclined individuals would complete the job.

When the state authorized a new penitentiary for the Eastern District of Pennsylvania in 1821, the Philadelphia reformers had a rather clear idea of what sorts of routines the physical structure of the prison would be expected to accommodate. They selected as architect a young English emigré, John Haviland. Haviland was well-trained but had

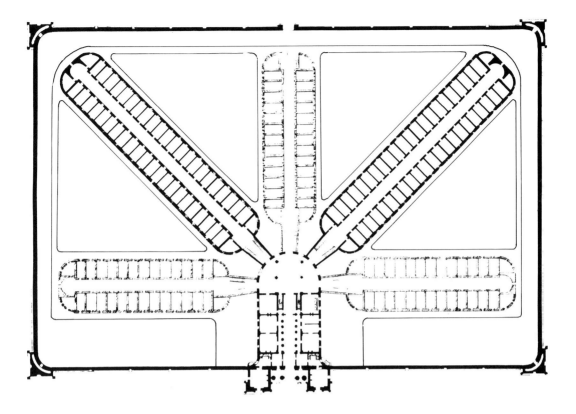

at that time only a passing interest in prisons.[23] He selected
a radial design for the prison in Philadelphia which in its
original conception was similar to the many county jails the
architect must have been familiar with in his native country. The early designs have not been located, but in his personal papers Haviland describes the original center building
as containing cells, laundry, bakery and a chapel above.
However, before the building was finished, Haviland had
made important modifications, utilizing for the first time
the real potential for surveillance of the hub-and-spoke or
radial layout. The prison was opened in 1829 and when completed several years later contained seven wings radiating
from a central rotunda. First floor cells had individual exercise yards and the cells themselves, which were of generous
proportions—8 x 12 feet x 10 feet high—contained hot water
heating, a water tap and toilet. Prisoners remained in their
cells during their entire sentence except for serious illness.

It is this prison of Haviland's, Cherry Hill as it was once
called, which became the point of controversy in the later
struggle with a rival American system and the institution
most often mentioned in penological writings. But two other
Haviland prisons were more important in influencing subsequent designs. These were the reconstructed Western
Penitentiary at Pittsburgh and the New Jersey State
Prison at Trenton, both erected in the 1830s. Pittsburgh was

in the form of a *V* with an inspection room at the apex. The Trenton plan, although not all its wings were built initially, consisted of five wings radiating from an inspection room in a half-circle radial pattern. It was to be the latter plan, which embodied improvements over Cherry Hill, such as detached exercise yards, cell doors into the corridors and two-story wings, which would be most widely imitated.[24]

Cherry Hill became, with the possible exception of the *maison de force* at Ghent, perhaps the first "successful" large-scale prison. This was hardly an accident. The Pennsylvania reformers had given the architect a very clear picture of what functions the prison building would be expected to embrace. Haviland, more than most prison architects before and after him, seemed to understand these functions as they were then conceived. He gave careful attention to details: floor paving stones were joined at points inaccessible to prisoners, and the entire array of cells was visible from a central watch tower as were the corridors from the room below. Much attention was given to the problem of illicit communication between prisoners, and standards of ventilation, heating and plumbing were to be seldom equaled in prisons during the ensuing 75 years.

Concerning style, the Building Commissioners had stated that "the exterior of a solitary prison should exhibit as much as possible great strength and convey to the mind a cheerless blank indicative of the misery which awaits the unhappy being who enters within its walls."[25] In the context of such a philosophy Haviland turned to the style of current English prisons, a heavy and gloomy Gothic. But the Cherry Hill facade was not in the elaborate and fussy style found in most European and American examples of Gothic. It was simple, restrained and massive.

From the time it was opened in 1829, the Eastern Penitentiary was a famous and controversial institution. When erected it was the largest and most expensive structure of any kind in America. Its dramatic architecture and its regimen of solitary confinement night and day became the subject of endless arguments, especially with the partisans of a rival system being developed in New York and Massachusetts. Although Haviland's prisons were never a direct major influence on American prison architecture, they became the prototypes for most of the prison buildings throughout the rest of the world during the 19th century. Soon after the first three cellblocks were completed at Cherry Hill and as Trenton was being built, the governments of Britain, France, Prussia, Russia, Belgium and several other nations sent representatives to evaluate the rival

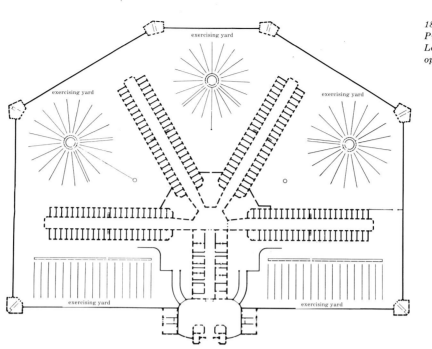

exercising yard

exercising yard

exercising yard

exercising yard

exercising yard

18. Pentonville Prison, London, opened 1842

19. Cell wing corridor, Strangeways Prison, Manchester, England, opened 1868

American experiments. Almost without exception, their reports favored the Pennsylvania System of solitary confinement and its associated architecture. It seems safe to assume that the high quality of the architecture which Haviland provided was one of the factors in the system's widespread acceptance.

Following a British report by William Crawford on United States prisons which was clearly partial to Cherry Hill and its system, Sir Joshua Jebb, an engineer and later one of the first Prison Commissioners, began a series of studies which resulted in the construction and opening of the Model Prison, later called Pentonville, in London in 1842. Two years later Reading Prison was completed and modifications and additions made at Preston. In these institutions the new system was begun, although with a certain amount of opposition. When prison construction in England, Scotland and Ireland stopped around the turn of the century, with two or three notable exceptions, all but the smallest structures were either built, rebuilt or modified to conform to layout principles and cellblock and cell standards established at

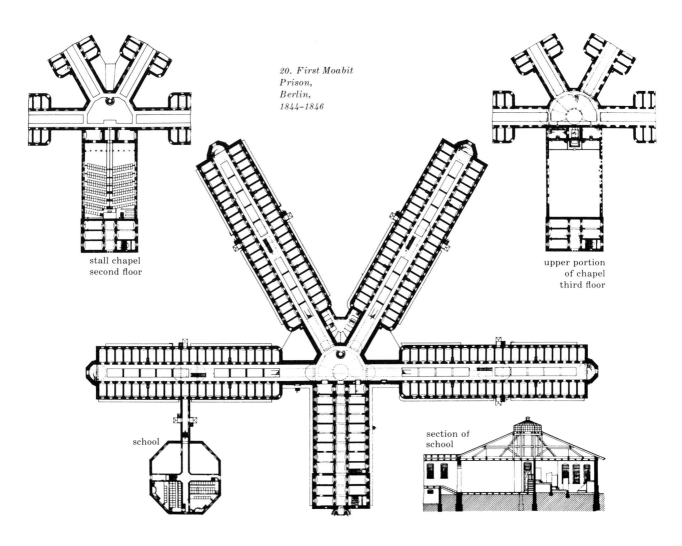

20. First Moabit
Prison,
Berlin,
1844–1846

stall chapel
second floor

upper portion
of chapel
third floor

school

section of
school

Pentonville.[26] Similar prisons continued to be built even later in other parts of the Empire such as Egypt, Australia, Malta, Burma and Canada.

The layout of the Model Prison was very similar to that of Trenton, as was most subsequent construction. Some few prisons contained five or six wings but most had four radiating from a rotunda. British prisons had common toilets and hot air heating but otherwise were similar in their details to the American prototypes. Individual exercise yards and chapels with stalls were provided to keep inmates separate at all times. Cells were usually on three or four levels, connected by balconies. These prisons continued to be built in a somber Gothic style but it became less exuberant – and less expensive – during the latter decades of building.

Pentonville, more accessible to Europeans than Trenton, became the most-copied prison in the world. In 1842 Frederick William IV of Prussia paid a visit with his architect Busse. He was followed shortly by the rulers of Saxony, Russia and the Netherlands, and commissioners from the governments of France, Austria, Holland, Denmark and Sweden. In each of these countries prototype prisons were eventually erected in the capital, patterned faithfully after Pentonville.

In Germany, for example, after an official visit by Dr. Nicolaus Julius to America and the King to England, a prison was opened in Berlin in 1844 in the Moabit district. A comparison of the London, Berlin and Trenton plans demonstrates the remarkably clear line of paternity. Shortly afterwards prisons were erected at Münster and Ratibor on cross plans. The Moabit and Ratibor plans became the two basic patterns for almost all subsequent 19th century prison building in the German states. Although a number of prisons, especially for long-term offenders, were located in old fortresses, over 40 radial prisons were erected in Germany before 1910.

Belgium, perhaps more than any other European country, completely replaced its old prisons in the last half of the 19th century, largely through the untiring efforts of one man, Edouard Ducpétiaux. A devotee of the Pennsylvania System and a student of English prisons, he made certain that most of the establishments erected during his long administration were radial in form. Some like Antwerp, Audenarde and Charleroi, were V-shaped like the second Pittsburgh prison; others were in an X-form, such as the great prison at Forest near Brussels. Still others, like Louvain and St. Giles, consisted of five or six wings radiating from a central rotunda, in a form more like the Cherry Hill plan. Only three of the over twenty new prisons erected in this country were not radial in the true sense.

Beginning with Vitoria prison in 1859, Spain began to build new provincial prisons which have, down to the present day, consistently been erected on the radial plan. The great "model prisons" in Madrid (1877) and Valencia (1887) were directly patterned after Pentonville, and Barcelona was built in a six-wing radial form. Altogether, over 40 major prisons have been erected on radial plans in Spain.

In the smaller countries of Western Europe, where but a few large prisons were erected, these were almost always patterned after Cherry Hill and Pentonville. The large prisons in Holland, Switzerland, the Scandinavian countries and Finland, Austria, Hungary and Portugal follow this pattern. Portugal, for example, built a large model prison in Lisbon in 1880, after Belgian models, with six wings radiating from a rotunda. Two other prisons at Coimbra and Santarém were later erected in cross forms. In France, Russia and Italy, political unrest, repeated financial problems and the ready availability of confiscated church properties which could be used as prisons resulted in few new prisons being erected except for purposes of detention. Those which were built were almost invariably faithful to the Pentonville layout as can be seen in the large prisons of

21. Kumamoto Prison, Japan, opened 1921

Mazas and Santé in Paris and Orléans in the provinces; in Italy at San Vittore in Milan, Regina Coeli in Rome and the detention prisons at Piacenza and Turin; or in Russia in the city prison at Piotrokow (Petrokof) and the great Viborg prison in St. Petersburg. A few long-term institutions were erected in these countries and in the familiar layouts — Civita Vecchia near Rome and Palermo, for example; or the Russian provincial prisons at Grodno, Lomja, Staraïa-Roussia, all based on model plans put forth by the prison administration and usually in a two- or three-wing pattern such as is found primarily in Belgium.

The various countries of Latin America have, with one or two exceptions, built few large central prisons until recent years. These early structures, usually erected in or near the capital, were almost always radial, reflecting either direct North American or British and Continental influences.

22. Typical Pennsylvania System individual exercise areas in 19th century German prison. Ends of wedge-shaped yards are enclosed with bars.

Argentina showed the greatest activity in 19th century prison building: the first of the new prisons, located at Buenos Aires (1872), was a classic five-wing radial. Others were erected on variations of this design.

One of the first effects which accompanied westernization of Japan was the advent of prison reform. Shikueya Ohara, a jurist and under-director of the prison administration, visited British colonial prisons and sent officials to America and Europe. The result was the enthusiastic adoption of cellular confinement and the acceptance of the radial prison plan as part of official policy.[27] The first of the new prisons,

*23. Rebibbia Prison,
Rome*

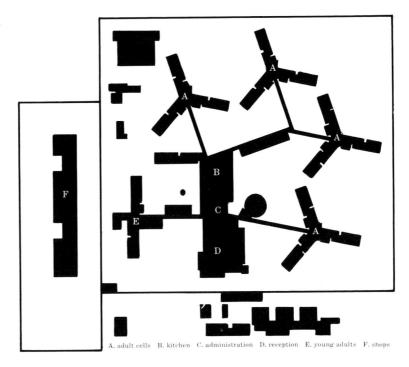

A. adult cells   B. kitchen   C. administration   D. reception   E. young adults   F. shops

Miyagi (1879), was designed by an English architect and consisted of six wings arranged very much like Louvain prison in Belgium. Over 33 radial prisons were erected in Japan until very recent years, the most common plan being based on Pentonville, as at Tokyo (1879), or occasionally five- or six-wing full circle radial designs, as at Gifu and Hakodate, opened in 1931. More true radial prisons were erected in Japan than in any other country, and only Belgium has rivaled her in the consistency of its prison architecture.

Reform came later in China and the first new prison was built in Peking in 1909 by a Japanese architect. Like many new prison structures put up in the following ten years, it consisted of a complicated array of three Trenton-type radial layouts, a three-wing *T*-form, and shop buildings.

The Pennsylvania System of solitary confinement upon which the foregoing examples were based was soon in trouble. Not only did it have an adverse effect on the mental and physical health of prisoners, but the cost of both buildings and maintenance was very high. Although the system was somewhat softened and modified, prisons continued to be built with separate exercise yards and stalls in chapels, and generally prisoners worked and exercised in silence through most of the 19th century in Europe. Well into the present century vestiges have remained of this system, and in many countries prisoners still eat in their cells and spend the initial months of their sentence in their cells.

The radial style itself was not quickly replaced in Europe. Spain has continued to construct a number of radial plan institutions, the largest of which is the post-Civil War penitentiary built in the suburbs of Madrid in the classic seven-wing radial plan. Italy is building by stages a huge prison complex in Rome known as Rebibbia, where recent cellhouses consist of four three-wing radial arrays. France has built a new prison in suburban Paris at Fleury-Mergolis which has five three-wing structures joined to a polygonal center building.

In the United States the radial plan had been used in a handful of 19th century institutions—the Philadelphia County Prison at Holmesburg (1895-1896), Rahway Reformatory, New Jersey, the Federal Penitentiary at Leavenworth, Kansas (1896-1928) to name a few. In recent years cellular living units at Lorton, Virginia, Moberly, Missouri, and Yardville, New Jersey, have featured three- or four-wing radial layouts.

The Haviland-inspired architecture has been dealt with at length because of its profound effect upon prison building in most parts of the world. However, the effect upon prison construction in the United States was minimal. The reason for this is closely tied with the establishment of an alternative system of prison treatment developed in New York state at Auburn and Sing Sing prisons.

Moving to relieve overcrowding in the old state prison on

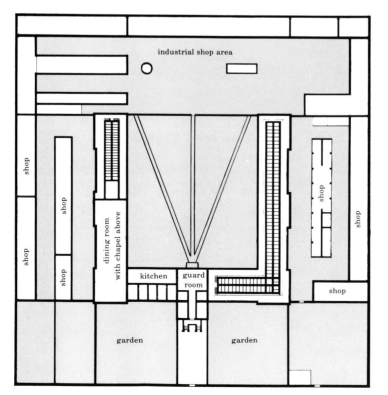

24. *Auburn Prison, opened 1817*

industrial shop area

shop

shop

dining room with chapel above

shop

shop

shop

kitchen

guard room

shop

garden

garden

Greenwich Street in New York City, the state began constructing a new prison at Auburn in 1816. The original wing was arranged according to the congregate system with rooms holding from two to ten prisoners. Following its opening there was considerable disorder and rioting, and consequently in the subsequent construction of a new cellblock a brief experiment with the Pennsylvania System was tried. Cells were 7½ feet x 3 feet 8 inches x 7 feet high, arranged back to back on five tiers in the center of a long cell building. Cell doors opened onto balconies facing a 9-foot-wide space open from ground level to ceiling. The wing was heated by stoves placed in the corridors and ventilated with ducts through which the prisoners communicated easily.

25. Inside cells of South Wing, Auburn Prison. The small dimensions of these early cells are evident.

The experiment in solitary confinement lasted three years but was abandoned because of the effect on the physical and mental health of the prisoners. The tiny cells were inadequate for work, there were no exercise yards and no outside visitors were permitted. A new warden, Elam Lynds, subsequently worked out what came to be called the Auburn System—congregate work in silence in the daytime in workshops, coupled with solitary confinement in sleeping cells at night. The Auburn System prevailed over the Pennsylvania System because the prison shops in the former had a higher level of inmate productivity than cell labor when the prisoner was isolated. The latter system was also more expensive to operate as it lacked inmate labor for housekeeping duties and the buildings were more expensive to construct. America, with its tradition of hard work and its chronic labor shortages, could not really tolerate the degree of relative idleness which Europeans would permit running their prison systems under the Pennsylvania regimen.

In 1825 prisoners arrived in leg shackles from Auburn at a site on the Hudson River, later to be known as Sing Sing, to construct a new prison. The plan was similar: tiny cells back to back on five tiers, with stairways on either end and in the center of the very long range. Cell doors were iron with grillework in the upper portion, and they fastened with gang locks. Cells received small amounts of light coming through a tiny window located 9 feet away in the outer wall opposite the cell door. These cells were extremely damp, dark and poorly ventilated and, like those at Auburn, contained no toilet facilities except buckets. The East House, which alone contained 1,000 cells and continued in use until 1943, was to become the prototype for most American prison cellhouse construction, rather than the earlier Auburn prison from which the system took its name.

For the remainder of the 19th century in this country, the characteristic layout for nearly all prisons was to consist of a central building housing offices, mess hall and chapel, usually flanked and joined on each side by a multitiered cellblock. In the prison enclosure formed by the wall would be shops, hospital and power plant. In 1834 Ohio opened a prison on this plan in Columbus. Five tiers of tiny cells (7 x 3½ x 7 feet) back to back were built with convict labor. Wisconsin opened a similar type of prison at Waupun in 1851. The Illinois Penitentiary at Joliet (1856-1858), the Rhode Island Penitentiary at Cranston (1873-1878), the Tennessee Penitentiary at Nashville (1895) and a number of others were on this plan. The largest prison of this sort was the Western Penitentiary at Pittsburgh (1882) with 1,100 cells on five tiers. A few such institutions were erected following the turn of the century—Cheshire, Connecticut, was opened in 1913 and Monroe, Washington, in 1908—but by that time nearly all the states had built maximum security prisons and little prison building would occur again until the 1930s.

Although in the early examples of the Auburn-style prisons cell partitions were of stone with wood and iron doors, the advances of technology and salesmanship led to increasing use of bars, doors, partitions, balconies and window sash made of steel. The characteristic inside maximum security cells of the Auburn System were particularly susceptible to the use of steel and iron bars and even steel partitions. Although heating and ventilating were immensely improved by these advances, privacy disappeared in these latter-day inside cells with barred fronts, peepholes in the rear wall opening to corridors between the backs of the cells, and a toilet in full view from the corridors. Ironically, technology and the vagaries of penal philosophy had brought the prisoner from the iron and wooden cages placed in the interior of medieval castles to steel cages lined up in the huge cellblocks of the American Auburn-type prisons.

These structures, as well as the few radial-type prisons which usually followed a similar internal regimen, continued to be built in a Gothic style.[28] By the second half of the 19th century these facades had taken on the curious Victorian "gingerbread" appearance of most city halls, schools, orphanages and hospitals of the time, so that the only thing which distinguished them as prisons was the high stone or concrete wall which invariably was attached.

20th Century Developments

The great rash of prison construction in the last half of the 19th century was followed by 30 years of relative inactivity. Two standard architectural solutions had been developed for handling large numbers of men in high security—the radial plan developed by Blackburn, Haviland and Jebb and common in most countries, and the system of flanking cell wings with inside cells which evolved in the Auburn System prisons in the United States. A third important plan developed which came to be called the "telephone-pole" or "telegraph-pole"—a series of parallel cellblocks, service facilities and shops flanking a long central corridor. It should be noted in passing that the third type of architecture was only that. The era of "systems" of penal treatment was past. The United States and European countries were henceforth to experiment with particular kinds of treatment strategies, none of which would ever come close to being regarded as an all-embracing panacea with an associated architecture as in the 19th century.

The evolution of the telephone-pole layout must be considered to have been inevitable. With the eclipse of the "systems", a moderate relaxation of the older discipline and an added use of vocational training, education and professional services resulted in increased movement of prisoners within the confines of the prison. A series of parallel pavilions arranged around a rectangular plot and connected by covered arcades had been used for large hospitals as early as the 18th century[29] and in 1839 the prison colony for youths at Mettray, France, was constructed on a similar plan. These institutions, however, must bear closer paternity to the open campus plan, to be discussed later, than to the high-security telephone-pole plan.

Because architects seldom write down their debts of inspiration, it is often difficult to know whether similarities of plan represent borrowing or are independently arrived at solutions. Although a French prison, Fresnes, is generally regarded as the prototype telephone-pole prison and without doubt was the inspiration for some latter-day institutions, the diffusion of this plan is not as well documented as the radial or Auburn. One institution must be mentioned which predates Fresnes by 24 years: Wormwood Scrubs, built in London from 1874 to 1891. A most notable departure from the Pentonville style, this prison was planned and erected under Sir Edmund DuCane, then chairman of the Prison Commissioners. It consisted of four parallel wings bisected by a narrow one-story passageway open to the weather on one side, and off which were also located workshops, service facilities and kitchen. There were 1,244 cells on four tiers, making it the largest prison in Europe for many years. This fact alone should have made prison architects in at least continental countries aware of its existence.

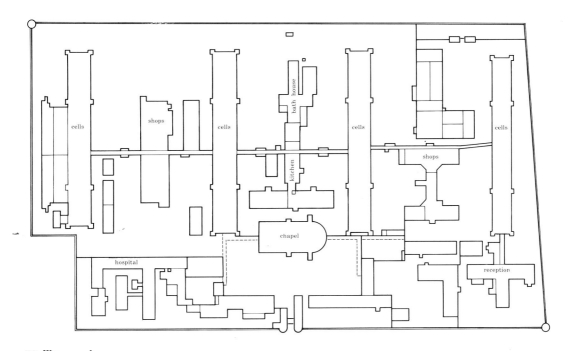

26. Wormwood
Scrubs Prison,
London, 1874–1891

The Seine Department prison at Fresnes-les-Ringis, on the outskirts of Paris, was designed by Francisque-Henri Poussin and opened in 1898. The architect grouped his six cellblocks together flanking a central corridor. Cells were on five levels with a total capacity of 2,000. Unlike Wormwood Scrubs, service facilities, chapel and administration buildings were located away from cell buildings but connected by corridors. Individual exercise yards were located in the space between the cell buildings.

27. Prison for the Seine Department, Fresnes, near Paris, opened 1898

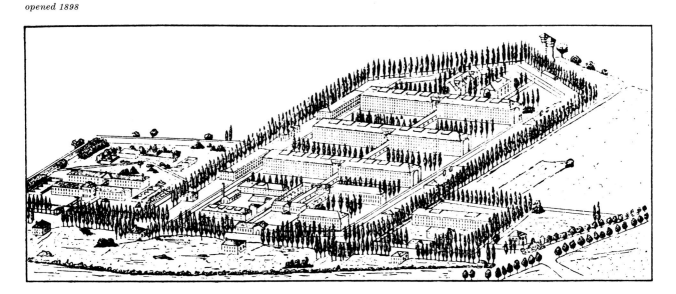

The United States was probably the first country to be influenced by the Fresnes layout. The State Prison at Stillwater, Minnesota (1913–1914), made partial use of the connecting corridor: flanking Auburn-type cell wings were connected to parallel wings containing services, a mess hall, chapel and an additional cellblock. Shops and other facilities were not connected however. An institution which came much closer to realizing the potentials of this plan was Kilby State Prison, Montgomery, Alabama, opened in 1922. Patterned after Stillwater, Kilby had three parallel blocks of outside cells, laundry and bathhouse, kitchen and mess hall and paper plant connected by a central corridor. Future buildings were to be joined to this corridor.

A variant on this plan was the state penitentiary erected at Graterford (1927–1928) near Philadelphia. Here five very long two-tiered cellblocks each contain 400 cells. Although shops, chapel, school and hospital are adjacent to the central corridor, the dining rooms and kitchen are at the opposite ends of the cell wings.

The man most frequently credited with bringing the telephone-pole plan to the United States was Alfred Hopkins.

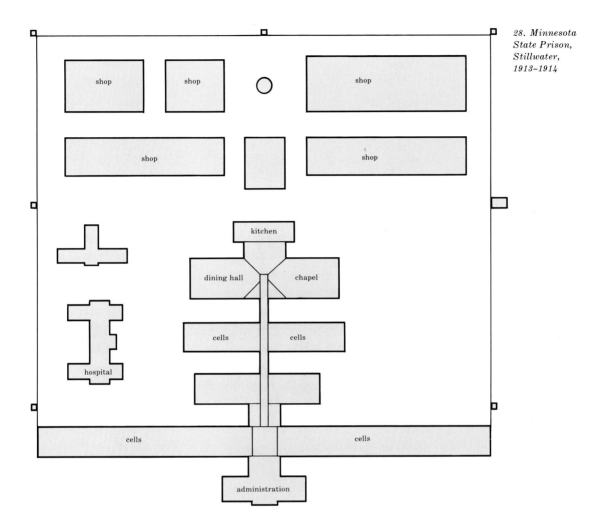

Whether the Fresnes plan was familiar to the architects of Stillwater, Kilby and Graterford is not known, but Hopkins, who had a long-standing interest in prison architecture, visited Fresnes and was aware of the Stillwater and Graterford plans when he designed the Federal Penitentiary at Lewisburg, Pennsylvania. Lewisburg opened in 1932 and, to a much greater extent than the three prior examples just described, seems to have been an effective vehicle for popularizing the telephone-pole plan with United States architects and prison administrators. Hopkins was a true pioneer in his efforts to break with some of the strong stylistic and other traditions of prison design. His first prison, Wallkill in New York state, was one of the first, if not the first, medium security prisons for adults. Although it was done in a "contemporary Gothic" style, its appearance was nothing like the older institutions, partly of course because it lacked a wall. Hopkins' other prisons, the Westchester Penitentiary at White Plains, New York, and the Berks County Prison at Reading, Pennsylvania, looked like college dormitories of the 1930s.

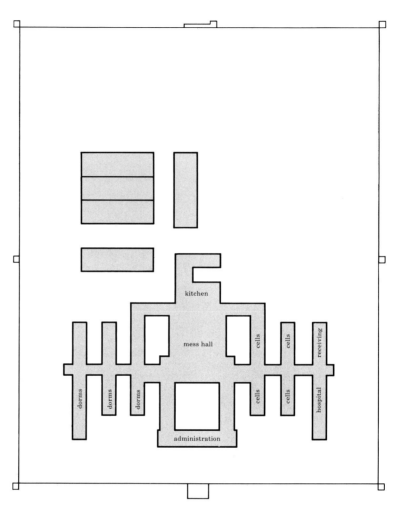

29. *United States
Penitentiary,
Lewisburg,
Pennsylvania,
opened 1932*

Lewisburg is built of red brick in a "northern Italian Gothic" style carried out on most of the interior details as well. Aside from its style, Lewisburg was innovative in being one of the first plans to incorporate different grades of security within the walled enclosure: there were maximum security inside cells, medium security outside cells, dormitories and "honor rooms". The Federal Bureau of Prisons regarded Lewisburg as ". . . perhaps the first institution in the history of prison construction in which the custodial facilities were built around classification and the fundamental fact that about seventy-five percent of even adult felons do not require maximum security housing."[30] Except for workshops, all other facilities of the prison were more or less adjacent to a connecting corridor.

As the passage quoted above indicated, the Federal Bureau was very favorably disposed towards the Lewisburg designs, so it was hardly a surprise that this plan was used in subsequent buildings. In later designs, however, refinements and improvements were made in Hopkins' basic layout in light of experience gathered from the operation of

Lewisburg. The telephone-pole plan was destined to become nearly the only one to be used for large high or medium security prisons in the United States and in some foreign countries for the next 40 years. El Reno, the Federal Reformatory in Oklahoma, was opened in 1934, a combination of telephone-pole wings and detached dormitories, all within a wire fence enclosure. At Terre Haute, Indiana, the Federal Penitentiary opened in 1940, also without a wall, contained a *V*-like arrangement of cellblocks at each end of the central corridor, thus effectively preventing overexpansion of housing units in the future.

Now many states, especially in the 1950s, embarked on construction replacing old, outmoded maximum security facilities. The rather routine application of the telephone-pole plan in the 1950s is exemplified by Soledad, Tracy and Vacaville in California; the New Mexico Penitentiary at Santa Fe; Marion and Lebanon Correctional Institutions in Ohio; Oregon State Correctional Institution, Salem; the Eastham Unit, Texas; Massachusetts Correctional Institution, South Walpole; Connecticut Correctional Institution at Osborn; and the Ontario Reformatory at Millbrook. In

30. Ohio Correctional Institution, Marion, opened 1955

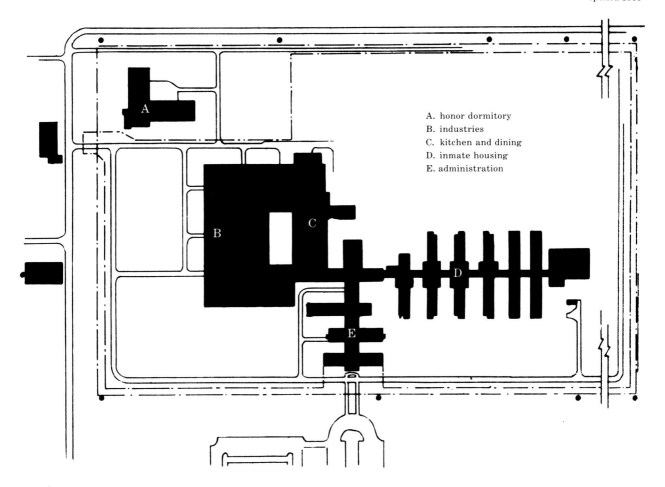

A. honor dormitory
B. industries
C. kitchen and dining
D. inmate housing
E. administration

some cases where this plan has been rather unimaginatively applied, the result, as pointed out by James V. Bennett, former Director of Federal Prisons, has been little flexibility in planning, too great emphasis on custody and, with a large institution, very long corridors. In the Texas maximum security prison for 1,500 opened in 1957, personnel used bicycles to get from one end of the corridor to the other.[31] Soledad in California has a 1,100-foot-long corridor off which are 1,500 cells.

One of the most useful modifications of the telephone-pole plan has been the use of corridor zones or completely separate areas, set off according to type of facilities or degree of custody of the living quarters. This cuts down on supervisory problems, makes possible the closing of some areas in the evening hours and the separation of different offender groups within one institution. In the federal prison at Marion, Illinois, opened in 1963, all facilities are off four corridors which join at a central control area at a level midway between the two-story wings in order to facilitate observation and traffic flow.

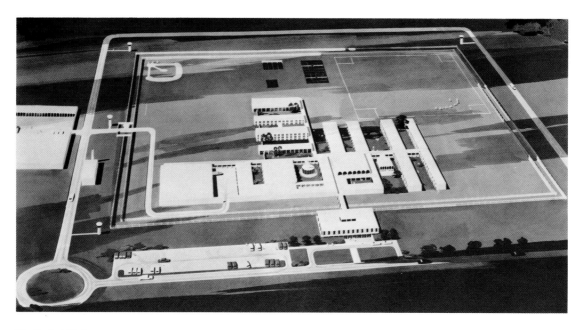

31. United States Penitentiary, Marion, Illinois, opened 1963

The Louisiana Penitentiary at Angola, opened in 1955, received a great deal of favorable evaluation. As can be seen from the accompanying illustration the prison is divided into areas based on function and security level as it must hold all the different types of adult male prisoners in the state. The maximum security portion contains cellblocks with two tiers of either inside or outside cells and is surrounded by a double wire mesh fence with towers. The other

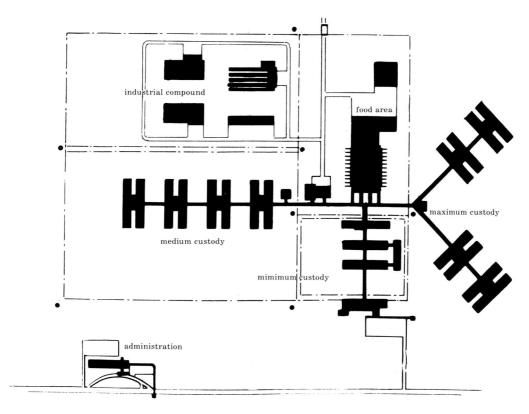

industrial compound

food area

maximum custody

medium custody

mimimum custody

administration

32. Louisiana State Penitentiary, Angola, opened 1955

two grades of security differ from each other only in the presence of a fence around the medium security area. Both utilize a "cloverleaf" plan, since adopted at Fox Lake, Wisconsin, and elsewhere, which consists of an *H*-shaped unit composed of four single-story dormitories joined to a center area containing baths and wash basins, and bisected by the connecting corridor which joins a series of such units.

Although after World War II the telephone-pole plan became the stereotyped solution to most all medium or maximum security prison buildings in the United States, it has been only occasionally used in other countries, partly because of the smaller size of their institutions. One of the rare examples of this type of institution to be constructed in the Orient was Yonago Prison, opened in 1923 in the western part of Honshu Island, Japan. Three cell wings were arranged on each of two corridors running at right angles to the wings and parallel with each other. Connected to these corridors and arrayed between them were adminstration building, bathhouse and kitchen. A number of relatively large telephone-pole-type prisons were built early in Latin America. The Cidade Penitentiary outside Rio de Janiero, Brazil (1937–1942), contains over 1,600 cells in eight wings off a central corridor. In Argentina, Venezuela, Paraguay and Ecuador a number of large prisons on similar plans—Latins call them "double comb" or "fish spine" plans — have been erected in recent years.

Brief mention should be made of another type of plan which enjoyed some brief though limited popularity in the 1930s and 1940s. Public buildings in the past have often been constructed in the form of a hollow, self-enclosed square. One of John Howard's model jail plans of the 1770s consisted of a rectangular array of six squares with open courts. But such a plan offered little appeal until the prison wall was dispensed with. Then the self-enclosing plan seemed like a secure substitute for the expensive wall. The state prison opened at Attica, New York, in 1931 had a wall but the cells were arranged in four blocks facing each other to form a very large square. The federal government built medium security institutions without walls at Milan, Michigan (o.1933), Danbury, Connecticut (o.1940), and Englewood, Colorado (o.1940), which were self-enclosed. Although not completely self-enclosed, the Michigan State Prison at Jackson (1924–1929) contains huge cellblocks on three sides with two walls joining the ends and enclosing 57 acres. There are over 5,700 individual cells.

Several institutions have combined elements of the self-enclosed plan and the telephone-pole plan, such as the Bordentown Reformatory, New Jersey (o.1936), Hopkins' Wallkill Prison (o.1933) and the more recent Pennsylvania Correctional Institution at Dallas (1956–1960). The hollow square in multiple arrays, somewhat formalistic in design, can be seen in the new prisons currently being built in Turkey and the Central Prison of the North at Porto, Portugal, and at Linhó outside Lisbon.

Architectural developments thus far traced have, with few exceptions, been variations on two basic housing schemes for prisoners developed well over a century ago — outside cells evolved in early institutions like San Michele (1704) and the Auburn-type inside cells found in Sing Sing and Auburn.

On the 19th century penal treatment systems were grafted in makeshift fashion various "reforms" of a humanitarian nature which tended to mitigate but not fundamentally alter the nature of the prison structure or the prison experience. Education, vocational training, classification, and various kinds of casework and evaluation by behavior specialists became part of most North American prisons in the 20th century. Concurrently, the rigors of 19th century prison life were considerably ameliorated. It was even discovered, partly it must be admitted due to increasing construction costs, that high security facilities were not necessary for the majority of prisoners.

But following World War II, some of the old optimism and self-confidence which had characterized American penology began to erode, accompanied by a slow but fundamental change in orientation. The reasons for this are not hard to find: with increasing systematic study by penologists and behavior scientists, some disconcerting things were being uncovered about the "new penology". The prison, with all its 20th century improvements, seemed to be still essentially the same ineffective, hit-and-miss instrument of social policy it had been from the beginning. The new techniques, when rigorously tested, turned out not to work very well, and one of the main causes was the existence of a homemade social system among the prisoners. This of course had always existed in varying degrees, but it turned out that its influence on the careers of inmates was much greater than the formal measures of rehabilitation.

With the increasingly demonstrated failure of classification, vocational and academic training, and limited psychological contacts to live up to expectations, coupled with the rediscovery of the importance of associations among prisoners, a new breed of career-oriented and educated correctional administrator began a determined search for new solutions. For the first time since the Pennsylvania and New York reformers of the early 19th century, planners and architects began to focus on the *inmate*, his contacts with fellow inmates, and now, how these contacts might be properly structured—rather than cut off—through new architectural devices.

Out of all of this came new kinds of correctional institutions for adults with layouts similar to those used heretofore only with juveniles or women. Freed from the preoccupation with security, architects have devised an architecture which must be regarded as much more significant than the telephone-pole structures or self-enclosed institutions already described. One of the earliest examples of the cottage or campus layout was the pioneer Mettray Colony built in France in the last century and described earlier. In such an arrangement, cottages or dormitories along with school, dining and other service facilities might be grouped formally along a central mall. Rectangular-shaped cottages or cell buildings were most commonly used. Perhaps the earliest clear example of this layout is the New Jersey Reformatory at Annandale (o.1929). Without a fence originally, this institution contains both dormitories and individual rooms. Algoa Farms, the Missouri Intermediate Reformatory at Jefferson City, opened in 1932, was modeled closely after Annandale. The Federal Correctional Institution at Seagoville, Texas (o.1940) is similarly laid out.

One of the earliest examples of a more informal arrangement was the Illinois women's prison at Dwight, opened in 1930. But beginning in the 1950s male institutions for young adults and even medium security facilities for adults began to appear in these informal arrays. These latter campus plans show more ingenuity than the more formal early examples. At the Michigan Training Unit at Ionia (o.1958) four living units are arranged around one side of a large open area and consist of two similar two-story wings forming a right angle and containing 60 outside rooms. Dayrooms and sanitary facilities are at the juncture of the two wings. The new unit of the Connecticut State Prison at Enfield, opened in 1960, has a similar layout except that the housing units consist of two three-wing structures along with a rectangular dormitory. In the Missouri Training Center for Men at Moberly (o.1963) there are four housing units in a St. Andrews cross-form, with offices, school, dining facilities and shops in between and beside them. In 1962 Wisconsin opened a correctional institution at Fox Lake. Within a fenced enclosure are six *H*-shaped housing units on the so-called "cloverleaf" plan. Each wing of these units has 24 outside rooms and a dayroom, with service facilities in the center. By using a masonry screen 3 feet from the exterior walls of the living units, no security windows were required. These institutions are only the first stirrings of the trend which is just beginning to take shape.

33. Wisconsin Correctional Institution, Fox Lake, opened 1962

Within the limits of space we have tried to trace the development of prison architecture from its antecedents in castle, dungeon and fortress, through the early little houses of correction and local prisons especially in Britain, to the rise of the Pennsylvania and Auburn systems with their very large, highly secure institutions, down to the 20th century telephone-pole prisons and the new breed of open, dispersed, minimum security facilities. The architects of prisons for adults up until very recent times had rather unambiguous demands made of them: to build a prison which was above all secure, which met minimum standards for sanitation and which would provide facilities for prisoners to work.

In the 19th century prison, a regimen so far removed from normal living was carried out that a series of complicated and unusual architectural arrangements were required. Even if workshops and work were available, prisoners remained in their cells for long periods of time and it was these little bedroom-dayrooms which, in large numbers, became the central core of the prison. The judicious and secure arrangement of those cells was the primary task of the architect. For the Pennsylvania System surveillance of cells where inmates spent most if not all of their time made the radial plan useful; for the Auburn System a series of living units near a number of workshops was typical. But as the size of prisons grew and the activities of prisoners aside from work and confinement in their cell increased, emphasis shifted away from the cell and its surveillance. It became necessary to provide plans to cope with the complicated and increased movements of prisoners about the prison. The telephone-pole plan appeared and possessed a particular kind of utility for large, secure institutions. During this time the earlier preoccupation with visual surveillance over everything all the time gave way partially to a new preoccupation with mechanical equipment and hardware as a way of containing and restraining the inmates. This proliferation of gadgetry is certainly predictable, given American technical competence, our long-standing love affair with things mechanical, and careful salesmanship campaigns mounted by manufacturers.

But by the 1940s, especially in the United States, a rather different sort of trend was becoming evident, evident but not overpowering yet. For a variety of reasons too complex to go into here, really new kinds of demands were being made on the architect. After a century of penological hand-wringing about the evils of size, there was now an increasing insistence that institutions be smaller. There was an

Conclusion

unmistakable veering away from the idea of maximum security for everybody towards the idea that most prisons need much less security. Only two walled prisons were built in North America after 1940.

This "new permissiveness" in penology has had rather dramatic if not entirely successful consequences for the architecture of penal institutions. During the exuberant period of prison reform in the late 18th and early 19th centuries, there existed a lively interest in prison architecture, a sanguine and sometimes naive faith in what it could achieve, and a participation by the best architects of the day in these experimental building ventures. But the period of vitality was followed by one of somnolence when a series of mediocre and inexperienced architects copied one another and the models of the past. Now, after generations of unimaginative duplication of first the radial, then the Auburn and finally the telephone-pole plans—at this point by unimaginative and entrenched architectural firms rather than individuals—correctional architecture seems to be once more entering into a period of innovation, vitality and creativity. This is demonstrated not only by some of the new institutions going up from Canada to Argentina, but by the fact that again first-rate architects are being drawn into competitions and planning, and that once more architects and penologists are sitting down and listening to each other.

The continual trend towards amelioration of the harshness of past prison life and the stress on normal living in groups, the use of much smaller institutions, and the increasing use of therapeutic techniques, have all resulted in the elimination of some of the prisonlike qualities of prisons.[32] But how far this trend will continue will depend on the community's willingness to support nonvindictive treatment programs and the eventual discovery of successful treatment techniques. But it also depends, in the immediate future at least, on some rather substantial contributions from the architect. If there is anything to be learned from this review of past prison building, it must certainly include the following points:

1) Prisons must be designed with a realistic understanding of the pressures and consequences of group living in institutions. This may mean consultations with not only the policy makers in administration but also guards and prisoners.

2) The large size of institutions may not be the main reason for their failure. But it is safe to assume that while a small prison is not certain to be successful, a large one *is* sure to be unsuccessful.

3) The dismal pattern presented on the preceding pages of stereotyped imitations and repetitions of fashionable plans must not continue. If anything is certain about correctional techniques over the next 20 years it is that they will change. This means that maximum flexibility must be provided for in every new design.

4) Undue reliance on ingenious plans, mechanical contrivances or structural innovations to effect rehabilitation, insure security or guarantee a smooth-running institution will only continue the long series of errors of the past. Human efforts can at best be aided, not supplanted, by such devices. The prison structure cannot be considered as the *deus ex machina* which will extricate us miraculously from the quicksand of prison practices.

5) Finally, the history of prison architecture stands as a discouraging testament of our sometimes intentional, sometimes accidental degradation of our fellow man. Prison structures have continued to be built in a way which manages by one means or another to brutalize their occupants and to deprive them of their privacy, dignity, and self-esteem, while at the same time strengthening their criminality. The 19th century allowed vast and dreary buildings and physical cruelty to grind down the prisoner. The contemporary prison seems to allow mechanical contrivances to dominate the prisoner. Architects in the future must share some responsibility for the unintended indignities made possible by their works.

The Illustrations

1. The Bastille (pg. 6)
   John Howard, from whose book
   the plan was taken, was one of
   the few prison reformers who
   ever got inside the infamous
   fortress-prison. Like many structures of its kind, it was basically
   military and administrative architecture whose apartments came
   to house political prisoners of
   rank and, during certain periods,
   ordinary criminals.
   John Howard, *State of the Prisons*,
   3rd ed. (London, 1784), plate 18,
   opp. pg. 174.
   Approximate scale:
   1 inch = 120 feet

2. Castle tower dungeon (pg. 7)
   Viollet-le-Duc, an architect and
   architectural historian of considerable reputation, had a special interest in castles. His
   meticulous restoration of Pierre-
   fonds, whose dungeons are
   shown in the illustration, was
   done for Napoleon III and can
   still be seen today.
   E. Viollet-le-Duc, *Dictionnarie
   raisonné de l'architecture*
   (Paris, n.d.), VII, pg. 482.
   Approximate scale:
   1 inch = 27 feet

3. San Michele, Rome (pg. 11)
   This structure, with almost no
   changes during the last 260 years,
   is still in use as a juvenile facility
   in Rome.
   Howard, *State of the Prisons*,
   plate 12, opp. pg. 114.
   Approximate scale:
   1 inch = 26 feet

4. Milan House of Correction (pg. 12)
   An early example of a well-planned
   workhouse used for minor offenders.
   Howard, *State of the Prisons*,
   plate 13, pg. 121.
   Approximate scale:
   1 inch = 34 feet

5. New Jail, Milan (pg. 14)
   This early 17th century structure
   is rather typical of the larger
   prisons with congregate housing
   of inmates in a rectangular arrangement of rooms.

Serafino Biffi, *Sulle antiche carceri di Milano* (Milan, 1884), plate 12.
Approximate scale:
1 inch = 48 feet

6. Newgate Prison, London (pg. 14)
A number of prisons bearing this name were built on the site of one of the early city gates. This old engraving seems to catch the spirit which, by all accounts, prevailed in most of the prisons of the 18th century. Note the sleeping cubicles and the lack of window glass.

7. Bentham's *Panopticon* (pg. 18)
This plan, one of several produced in conjunction with an architect, was never built in Britain during Bentham's lifetime. It is evident from his writings that this was one of his most deeply felt disappointments.
Jeremy Bentham, *Works,* ed. by John Bowring (Edinburgh, 1843), IV, opp. pg. 172.
Approximate scale:
1 inch = 24 feet

8. Illinois State Penitentiary, near Joliet (pg. 19)
This prison, usually referred to as Stateville, was built with inmate labor. The photograph clearly shows the four *Panopticon* cellhouses surrounding a circular mess hall. The large rectangular wing was added later. Aerial photographs such as this have not been permitted until recent years.
Illinois Department of Corrections

9. Cellhouse, Illinois State Penitentiary, (pg. 19)
This photograph reveals the large amount of wasted space inherent in the *Panopticon* design. An added liability, from the standpoint of security, is that while the guards can see all the prisoners, the prisoners can easily follow the movements of the guards as well.
Illinois Department of Corrections

10. Virginia Penitentiary, Richmond (pg. 20)

Designed by Benjamin Latrobe
and Thomas Jefferson, the prison's plan was heavily influenced
by a French architect friend of
Jefferson and by the several
semicircular prisons in Britain
which Latrobe must have been
aware of prior to his emigration
to America. This rare old photograph shows the prison some
years after its reconstruction
following a fire in 1823.
Virginia Division of Corrections
and Professor Ruth Shonle Cavan.

11. County Jail, Ipswich (pg. 22)
This is one of the earliest cruci-
form prisons, developed by
Blackburn, which permitted
visual inspection from the center.
Approximate scale: Not known

12. Abingdon Jail (pg. 22)
This photograph is of the jail as
it appeared in 1959, at which time
it was used as a grain storehouse.
A sense of the scale of these early
radial prisons is apparent.
Abingdon Town Clerk, Mr. E.W.J.
Nicholson and Ivor Fields,
photographer.

13. House of Correction,
Bury St. Edmunds (pg. 23)
The Bury prison was regarded as
a model for the period. The plan
provided for separation of males
from females, convicted from
those awaiting trial, and debtors
from misdemeanants and felons.
The detached center building for
the keeper or warden offered only
limited opportunities for visual
surveillance of cell wings.
John Orridge, *Description of the
Gaol at Bury St. Edmunds* (London, 1819), plate 1, opp. pg. 32.
Approximate scale:
1 inch = 53 feet

14. Petite Roquette, Paris (pg. 24)
This prison was large for its time
and is still in use to house women
offenders. No visual inspection of
corridors was possible from the
center building, which was connected by cast iron bridges to the
upper stories of the cell wings.
Professor Ruth Shonle Cavan.

15. Gothic facade, Leicester (pg. 27)
Typical of the smaller British
prisons built before the American
architectural influence
of the 1840s.
British Central Office of
Information, London.

16. Eastern Penitentiary,
Philadelphia (pg. 29)
This 1855 engraving by a prisoner,
identified only by number, clearly
shows the three single-story and
four two-story wings of
Haviland's prison before later
additions. All through the 19th
century this prison was called
Cherry Hill, having been built in
a former orchard.
*Pennsylvania Journal of Prison
Discipline*, Vol. XI
(April, 1856), opp. pg. 65.

17. New Jersey State Prison,
Trenton (pg. 30)
When the prison opened in 1836
only the two front wings had
been built. It is still in use.
F. A. Demetz & G. Abel Blouet,
*Rapports sur les pénitenciers des
États-Unis* (Paris, 1837),
plate 31, pg. 63.
Approximate scale:
1 inch = 58 feet

18. Pentonville Prison, London (pg. 32)
Except for the exercise yards and
the absence of one cell wing, the
plan is very similar to the Trenton plan. Its designers had carefully studied Haviland's Philadelphia and Trenton structures.
Great Britain, *Fourth Report of
the Inspector of Prisons* (London,
1839), plate 2, opp. pg. xvi.
Approximate scale:
Not known

19. Strangeways Prison,
Manchester (pg. 32)
The photograph conveys the
gloom which is so characteristic
of the interiors of the
19th century prisons.
British Prison Commissioners.

20. Moabit Prison, Berlin (pg. 33)
This prison, strikingly similar in
plan to Pentonville and Trenton

prisons, was the prototype for much of the German building in the second half of the 19th century.
Karl Krohne & R. Uber, *Die Strafanstalten und Gefängnisse in Preussen* (Berlin, 1901), Atlas, plate 62.
Approximate scale:
1 inch = 91 feet

21. Kumamoto Prison, Japan (pg. 35)
This facility is typical of the radial prisons erected in Japan on American and European models from 1879 until 1936.
Mr. Fujitaro Kusunoki, Bureau of Correction, Japanese Ministry of Justice.

22. Individual exercise yards, Germany (pg. 36)
Most European 19th century prisons had provisions for individual exercise yards in order to preserve a measure of separation of prisoners according to a modified Pennsylvania System of solitary confinement. Sometimes these enclosures were rectangular and arranged in rows; other times they consisted of fan-shaped or circular arrays, usually with an inspection cubicle for a guard located at the hub. Some of these yards still exist in Belgian prisons though they are now unused. They are referred to as "Lions' Cages".
Professor Ruth Shonle Cavan.

23. Rebbibia Prison, Rome (pg. 37)
A contemporary use of radial cell wings.
United Nations, Social Defence Research Institute, *Prison Architecture* (Rome, 1970), n.p.
Approximate scale:
1 inch = 195 feet

24. Auburn Prison, New York (pg. 38)
Cells were constructed at various times between 1820 and 1835 with several master builders, architects and wardens responsible for their design. Both the system of

discipline and the inside cellblocks developed over this period
came to be prototypes for most
of the subsequent American prisons of the 19th century.
William Crawford, *Report on the
Penitentiaries of the United States*
(London, 1835), appendix, opp. pg.
23. Reproduced by permission of
Patterson Smith Publishing
Corporation, publishers of 1969
reprint edition.
Approximate scale:
1 inch = 121 feet

25. Inside cells, Auburn
    Prison (pg. 39)
    These cells were for sleeping only.
    They were unheated, had no
    plumbing and received little
    light or air through the heavy
    double doors which opened on
    galleries or balconies.
    U. S. Bureau of Prisons, *Hand-
    book of Correctional Institution
    Design and Construction* (Leaven-
    worth, Kansas, 1949), pg. 9.

26. Wormwood Scrubs Prison,
    London (pg. 42)
    The British finally broke away
    from the radial tradition with a
    design anticipating Fresnes and
    the telephone-pole plan.
    British Prison Commissioners.
    Approximate scale:
    1 inch = 210 feet

27. Fresnes Prison, near Paris (pg. 43)
    This famous prison is generally
    regarded as the parent of the
    telephone-pole plan, which has
    dominated world prison
    building during the first half
    of this century.

28. Minnesota State Prison,
    Stillwater (pg. 44)
    A very early example of the
    Fresnes plan in the United States.
    Alfred Hopkins, *Prisons and
    Prison Building*
    (New York, 1930), pg. 54.
    Approximate scale:
    1 inch = 186 feet

29. United States Penitentiary,
    Lewisburg, Pennsylvania (pg. 45)
    This prison, the best-known early
    example of the telephone-pole

plan in America, embodies a clear break from the ponderous styles of the 19th century prisons and made its architect, Alfred Hopkins, famous.
U. S. Bureau of Prisons, *Handbook*, pg. 72.
Approximate scale:
1 inch = 190 feet

30. Ohio Correctional Institution, Marion (pg. 46)
Typical high security prison on the telephone-pole plan. Many prisons like this were erected in the 1950s in the United States.
U. S. Bureau of Prisons, *Recent Prison Construction 1950–1960* (Leavenworth, 1960), pg. 43.
Approximate scale:
1 inch = 370 feet

31. United States Penitentiary, Marion, Illinois (pg. 47)
This prison, originally designed to replace Alcatraz, was completed without the intended surrounding wall. It represents a determined attempt to break away from the more traditional architectural treatment of very high security facilities.
Hellmuth, Obata, & Kassabaum Inc., Architects, San Francisco, California.

32. Louisiana State Penitentiary, Angola (pg. 48)
One of the earliest attempts to provide varied degrees of custody in a unified plan. Like the federal facility at Marion, Illinois, it represents a turning away from conventionally used forms and materials in prison building.
U. S. Bureau of Prisons, *Recent Prison Construction*, pg. 31.
Approximate scale: Not known

33. Wisconsin Correctional Institution, Fox Lake (pg. 51)
The so-called campus plan, individual buildings dispersed over a large plot, has come to be characteristic of most recent medium and minimum security construction.
The American Foundation Institute of Corrections

Notes

1. Prisons are mentioned in the historical records of ancient Japan, China, Egypt and Greece, and in the latter Empire period are noted in the Roman law. In literature and folklore, as well, they are mentioned as existing during very early periods of civilization. The *Shu Ching,* a collection of Chinese poetry, history and philosophy, edited by Confucius, notes the building of prisons by the Emperor Fuen VIII about 2000 B.C. (*Le Chou-King, un des livres sacrés des Chinois,* trans., by Joseph de Guignes, [Paris, 1770], pg. 72.)

2. Ralph B. Pugh, *Imprisonment in Medieval England* (Cambridge, 1968), esp. Chap. 1. This work gives a very detailed picture of early imprisonment and conditions during the medieval period.

3. For a greater exposition of this view, see Thorsten Sellin, "Penal Servitude: Origin and Survival", *Proceedings of the American Philosophical Society,* Vol. 109, No. 5 (Oct., 1965).

4. Gotthold Bohne, *Die Freiheitsstrafe in den Italienischen Stadtrechten des 12.-16. Jahrhunderts* (Leipzig, 1922), I, pg. 78.

5. "Mamertine Prison", *Builder* (London), XXXIII (July 3, 1875), pg. 593.

6. A. Hamilton Thompson, *Military Architecture in England During the Middle Ages* (London, 1912), pg. 146.

7. A 14th century Carthusian house known as Mount Grace had a series of walled enclosures 27 feet square around a central cloister. Each contained a little two-story house for a monk providing a living room with fireplace, a small bedroom, a study and a workroom. There was a garden, a privy and piped water, and the monk might work and meditate with no contacts with the outside.

8. William Dugdale, *Monasticom Anglicanum* (London, 1817), I, pg. 218.

9. F. A. Karl Krauss, *Im Kerker vor und nach Christus* (Freiburg, 1895), pg. 331.

10. Thorsten Sellin, *Pioneering in Penology* (Philadelphia, 1944), pgs. 102–110.

11. The *Malefizhaus* built in Bamberg, Germany, in 1627, was a two and a half story structure, which contained cells for witches, sorcerers and "sinners" In 1677 a cellular hospice was opened in Florence for delinquent boys. It should also be noted in considering the architectural antecedents of the prison cell that hospitals, particularly plague hospitals or lazarettos, were often built in a cross-form or hollow square, with individual rooms.

12. John Howard found 540 prisoners in eight rooms in the Vicaria, a large prison in Naples, in the late 18th century.

13. Although Wood Street was closed as a prison in 1790, three or four of the underground vaults remain intact. Each is approximately 25 feet long, 13 feet wide and 9 feet to the crown of the arch. Little holes in the ceiling about a foot in diameter provided ventilation.

The underground portion of Warwick consists of an octagonal vaulted structure 21 feet in diameter and 19 feet below the surface. In the center is a small open cesspool. As many as 59 persons were confined there at one time, necessitating their lying side by side.

14. The writer's translation of a quotation from Cerdán de Tallada cited in Fernando Cadalso, *Instituciónes penitenciarias y similares en España* (Madrid, 1922), pg. 165.

15. *Principj* (Venezia, 1785), II, pgs. 227–228. Translation by the writer.

16. *Prisons with the 'Carceri' Etchings by G. B. Piranesi* (Los Angeles, n.d.), pg. xiii.

17. Thomas H. Shepherd, *Modern Athens Displayed in a Series of Views or: Edinburgh in the Nineteenth Century* (London, 1831), pg. 59.

18. Great Britain, *Fifth Report of the Inspectors General on the Prisons of Ireland*, 1826–1827, British Sessional Papers, Vol. XI, pg. 7.

19. Great Britain, *Report of the Surveyor-General of Prisons on the Construction, Ventilation and Details of Pentonville Prison, 1844* (London, 1844), pg. 8.

20. "Prisons", *Encyclopedia Londinensis*, Vol. XXI (London, 1826), pgs. 421–422.

21. Quoted in J. A. Picton, *Memorials of Liverpool* (Liverpool, 1907), II, pg. 44.

22. *An Account of the Principal Lazarettos in Europe* (London, 1789), pg. 78.

23. Haviland's uncle, a member of the Russian court, was a friend of John Howard and Haviland's mentor in England is known to have designed at least one prison. Haviland's participation in the competition for the penitentiary designs was clearly part of his early, general professional enthusiasm, rather than a special interest.

24. There is some indication that Haviland himself regarded Trenton as superior. He once described it as his prison "most worthy of copying", according

to a letter written to the French commissioners,
Demetz and Blouet (Haviland Papers, Journal No.
3, MSS, University of Pennsylvania Library).

25. *Book of Minutes of the Building Commissioners,*
bound MSS in Archives of Eastern
Penitentiary, pg. 115.

26. The pace at which construction proceeded during
this period is evident from the statement of one of
the early chairmen of the Prison Commissioners
that, within six years after Pentonville was erected,
54 new prisons with a total of 11,000 cells were constructed following its general design (Edmund F.
DuCane, *The Punishment and Prevention of Crime*
[London, 1885], pg. 56).

27. In 1883 a disastrous fire at Hiroshima prison
caused a temporary shift of policy to isolated
parallel blocks, but after five years this plan was
abandoned as too inconvenient, and radial plans
were again used.
The writer is indebted to the Japanese Ministry
of Justice, and especially Mr. Fujitaro Kusunoki,
architect of the Bureau of Correction, for much of
the information in the text concerning Japan, as
well as for a series of plans and photographs of
prisons. Details of only a few of these prisons
have ever appeared in European or English
language sources.

28. A conscious attempt at period style was confined
to the front facade of the prison or the administration building usually. Buildings screened by high
prison walls were in a more spartan style. In fact
the old blocks at Sing Sing had a kind of lean stark-
ness which almost seems to anticipate the Bauhaus
and more modern genres.

29. Hans Pfeiffer, "Neuzeitliche Gefängnisbauten
und ihre Geschichte", *Blätter für Gefängniskunde*,
LXV (1934), 2nd Sonderheft, pgs. 94–95.

30. U. S. Bureau of Prisons, *Handbook of Correctional
Institution Design and Construction* (Leavenworth,
Kansas, 1949), pg. 72.
The first portion of this statement is either an
excess of enthusiasm or simply bad history: the
many jails and prisons built from the 1780s in
Britain were planned with a very definite system
of classification of prisoners in mind. It is only after
the "systems" of the 19th century prevailed that
this practice was abandoned. It might also be noted
that in the very earliest jails in Britain there were
clear differences in security in different portions
of the jail structure and different kinds of prisoners
were lodged there. (See Pugh, *op. cit.*, especially
Chaps. 10 and 15.)

31. U. S. Bureau of Prisons, *Recent Prison Construction 1950–1960* (Leavenworth, Kansas, 1960), pg. 2.

32. Very early in the game, architects began to use a castle-like Gothic style for prisons. This became nearly invariable in both the Auburn- and the Pennsylvania-inspired prisons and even in some of Hopkins' 20th century institutions, though by this time the style was lighter and less elaborate. The 20th century telephone-pole or Auburn prisons without a wall have been as devoid of a distinctive style as a warehouse. But with more normal living and working arrangements for inmates in contemporary minimum security institutions, the style became little different from that of a residential school. More ordinary building materials, greater use of glass, lively colors and more informal, smaller living units characterize these new facilities.

About the Author

When The American Foundation in Philadephia received a request from the Law Enforcement Assistance Administration to prepare a developmental history of correctional architecture we began to telephone universities throughout the land. "Who," we asked, "is an able man on the subject?" From everywhere the same answer came back to us, "Norman Johnston, of course." So we made a local call to suburban Beaver College and this book is the result.

Dr. Johnston's interests in corrections go back to his college days in Michigan when he did practice teaching and lived in the warden's house at the old Michigan State Reformatory at Ionia. After graduation he worked as a staff sociologist in the Illinois prison system. He took leave from Illinois to do graduate work at the University of Pennsylvania. There Thorsten Sellin suggested that he do some research on prison architecture, and he did.

Later as a Fulbright fellow he traveled to England, Italy, and Spain where he studied old documents, visited old prisons and recorded much of the rare historical material contained in this

Photograph of William Nagel and Norman Johnston by George Krause

book. The Spanish visits were especially fascinating. Each started with a glass of sherry with the director followed by the most detailed of prison tours. "I had to see every storeroom, every dental chair, every toilet, every cell, even every women's section," he recalls. That was in 1959.

His interest in prison architecture has never diminished. The late Negley Teeters, another inveterate world traveler in pursuit of correctional knowledge, encouraged Johnston to even deeper expertise in the subject. He added some unlikely advice for a professor in these days of "publish or perish": "Don't worry about publications and career influence. You enjoy this. Keep digging around. See it. Write about it. Somehow it will get published." Dozens of his articles have and now this short book.

Johnston has a Doctor of Philosophy degree from the University of Pennsylvania where he taught for several years. He is now Professor and Chairman of the Department of Sociology and Anthropology at Beaver College in Glenside, Pennsylvania.

Designed by: Samuel Maitin, assisted by Deborah Seideman
Printed by: Consolidated/Drake Press, Philadelphia, Pa.
Typesetting by: Graphic Arts Composition, Inc.